Reading Success

Book 3

By
Celia Stone, Elizabeth Franks, & Myra Nicholson

Cover Design by
Terri Moll

Inside Illustrations by
Julie Anderson

Publisher
LDA
a division of Instructional Fair Group
a Tribune Education Company
Grand Rapids, Michigan 49544

LDA

LDA grants the right to the individual purchaser to reproduce patterns and student activity materials in this book for noncommercial individual or classroom use only. Reproduction for an entire school or school system is strictly prohibited. No other part of this publication may be reproduced in whole or in part. No part of this publication may be reproduced for storage in a retrieval system, or transmitted in any form or by any means, electronic, mechanical, recording, or otherwise, without the prior written permission of the publisher. For information regarding permission write to: LDA, Instructional Fair Group, P.O. Box 1650, Grand Rapids, MI 49501.

Credits:
Authors: Celia Stone, Elizabeth Franks, Myra Nicholson
Project Director: Sherrill B. Flora
Editors: Sherrill B. Flora, Karen Seberg
Special Education Consultants: Patricia Ann Seldon
Cover Design: Terri Moll
Inside Illustrations: Julie Anderson
Text Design: River Road Graphics

Standard Book Number: 1-56822-935-6
Reading Success—Book 3
Copyright © 2000 by LDA
a division of Instructional Fair Group
a Tribune Education Company
3195 Wilson Drive NW
Grand Rapids, Michigan 49544

All Rights Reserved • Printed in the USA

Preface

If your child or student is struggling to read, write, and spell, this book will help you. It has been designed to be used by teachers, parents, or tutors who have no specialist training in the teaching of dyslexic students.

As co-authors we are two teachers and a teacher/speech therapist who, after a long association with children with specific learning difficulties or dyslexia, decided to put together in book form, a collection of our most interesting and successful teaching materials. We have gleaned ideas from many sources and built on them in a carefully structured multisensory form, using a "seeing, saying, listening, writing" approach. We have used the work of our predecessors in the field, Gillingham/Stillman/Orton, Hickey, Cowdrey, and others whose methods have become the foundation of this kind of teaching.

The program has been developed over a number of years and has been successful in its present form as the main scheme of work in the Dyslexia Units at Bronte House School, Bradford, at Clevedon House, Ilkley, and in the Speech and Language Unit at Fir Tree Middle School, Leeds, England. It has also been particularly successful with a number of students having individual tutoring.

This is the third in a series of workbooks designed to take students progressively from the very first stages of letter recognition to full literacy. It is a **"reading through spelling"** program and ensures that the problems of spelling and writing are overcome as the child learns to read.

We realize that one of the problems is a short attention span and we have therefore made every effort to ensure that the exercises are as varied and entertaining as possible.

Foreword

It is accepted worldwide that in teaching literacy skills to dyslexics, the most effective approach is to use structured multisensory methods. There is no magic in this teaching process, just good psychological principles applied rigorously to the practice of learning by both teacher and student.

The basic underlying principles were derived by the world famous psychologist, Samuel Orton and used very positively in the Orton, Gillingham, Stillman method which, from its publication almost fifty years ago, became the accepted international teaching approach.

I have it on the very good authority from a former close colleague of Sam Orton's that, while traveling in the Malay States in the 1930s, he spent some time as a guest on a rubber plantation. While wandering through the station he was stopped in his tracks by the sight of a very skillful teacher working with a large group of over 100 newly recruited Chinese laborers. The laborers had to achieve a standard functional literacy in English very quickly, so that they could receive instructions and discharge their duties in that language.

The teacher was making this large group of students look at the letter shape, say the sound, and then trace with their hands in the air the moving pattern needed to write the letter. Orton was very impressed with the psychological appropriateness of a method which linked shape, sound, movement pattern, and meaning so efficiently for the learner. He had the creativity to appreciate that this technique offered a very effective solution to the literacy learning problems experienced by dyslexics.

When he returned to the U.S.A., he collaborated with Anna Gillingham and Bessie Stillman to establish the teaching approach which, over the years, has been demonstrated to be so successful with these learners. Since then, structured multisensory methods have become the key approach in teaching literacy skills to dyslexic students.

Orton's original methods, which were documented in great detail in the original Orton/Gillingham/Stillman manual, have been greatly refined over the years and are now acknowledged internationally to be a very efficient teaching tool. These methods are central to the approach taken in *Reading Success* and are of great value in enabling dyslexic students to develop more effective literacy competencies. The material in this book is relevant and will be of value for classroom and specialized teachers who seek to use psychologically appropriate methods in their teaching of dyslexics.

Dr. H.T. Chasty, Ph.D.

Table of Contents

Preface and Foreword... 3

Tutorial for All Users, Teachers, and Parents 7
    Materials Needed.. 8
    Introduction... 9
    Alphabet Arc... 10–11
    Auditory and Visual Introductions............................... 12
    Listen to the Teacher (Transcript for Auditory Exercises)...... 13–15
    Reading Pack and Sound Picture/Spelling Pack................. 16–18
    Instant Words... 19
    Reading Games for Instant Words............................. 19–20
    Controlled Vocabulary.. 20
    Word Families and Rhyming..................................... 20
    Grammar... 21
    Irlen Syndrome (Scotopic Sensitivity Syndrome).................. 21
    Record Page... 21
    To Sum Up... 21
    Conclusion... 21
    Reproducible Caterpillar Record Page............................ 22
    Manuscript Uppercase Chart.................................... 23
    Manuscript Lowercase Chart.................................... 24
    Cursive Uppercase Chart....................................... 25
    Cursive Lowercase Chart....................................... 26
    Lined Practice Sheet.. 27

The Lessons 29
    What Do You Remember from *Book 1* & *Book 2*?................ 30
    Finding Out What You Know..................................... 31
    Consonant Digraph –NG –ng.................................... 32
    More About Consonant Digraph –NG –ng........................ 33
    More About Consonant Digraph –NG –ng........................ 34
    Words Ending in –nd –nt –nk –ng................................ 35
    More –nd –nt –nk –ng Endings.................................. 36

    Puzzle Words.. 37
    Alphabetical Order.. 38

    Consonant Digraph TH th....................................... 39
    More About Consonant Digraph TH th........................... 40
    More About Consonant Digraph TH th........................... 41

    Essential Spellings.. 42
    More About th and f.. 43
    Instant Words... 44
    Verbs and the Ending –ing...................................... 45

    Consonant Digraph –CK –ck.................................... 46
    More About Consonant Digraph –CK –ck........................ 47
    More About Consonant Digraph –CK –ck........................ 48
    Short Vowels Followed by –ck................................... 49
    –ck or –k at the End of 1 Syllable Words......................... 50
    More About –CK or –k... 51

Handwriting Practice.	52
Play Hockey with Stubby's Team	53
Sound Pictures → Words	54
Syllable and Vowel Consonant Patterns	55
V / V C Pattern	56
Puzzle Words	57
Letter Vv — a consonant	58
More About Letter Vv	59
More About Letter Vv	60
Letter Ww — a consonant	61
More About Letter Ww	62
More About Letter Ww	63
Handwriting Practice.	64
Essential Spellings	65
Instant Words	66
There and Their	67
Letter Jj — a consonant	68
More About Letter Jj	69
More About Letter Jj	70
Alphabetical Order.	71
Letter Yy — a consonant	72
More About Letter Yy	73
Question Words.	74
More About Long Vowels	75
More About Long Vowels	76
Consonant Digraph SH sh	77
More About Consonant Digraph SH sh	78
More About Consonant Digraph SH sh	79
Storybook — Crisis for the Pilot	80–81
Handwriting Practice.	82
Flag Design	83
Nouns.	84
Letter "a" Saying ◆	85
Storybook — Winston and Wilfred Go to the Windmill	86–88
Sound Pictures → Words.	89
Essential Spellings	90
Word Families and Rhyming	91
Word Families and Rhyming	92
Letter Qq — a consonant	93
More Combination QU qu.	94
More About QU qu	95
The Doubling Rule	96
Suffixes and the Doubling Rule.	97

Letter Xx — a consonant 98
More About Letter Xx 99
More About Letter Xx 100

The Past Tense of the Verb 101
More About Suffix –ed 102
More About Suffix –ed 103

Sound Pictures → Words 104

Punctuation 105
Storybook — Help! A Bad Dog 105–108

Letter Zz — a consonant 109
More About Letter Zz 110
More About Letter Zz 111

Capital Letters 112
Adjectives 113
Alphabet Review 114
Handwriting Practice 115

Final –ff 116
More About ll, ss, ff, ck 117
More About ll, ss, ff, ck 118

Storybook — Hugo the Tulip Addict 119–122
Game — Stubby's Cross Country Run 123–124

Consonant Digraph — CH ch 125
More About Consonant Digraph — CH, ch 126

Storybook — Max and His Gang of Chimps 127–129
Handwriting Practice 130
How Much Have You Learned? 131
How Much Have You Learned? 132
Word Race. Beat the Clock 133

Certificate of Merit 134

Appendix A 135
   Reading & Sound Pictures/Spelling Pack Vowels 137–140
   Reading Pack Consonants 141–144
   Sound Pictures/Spelling Pack 145–148

Appendix B 149
   Phonetic Word Flash Cards 150–170
   Question Words 171
   Instant Word Flash Cards 172–176

How to Use This Book

Tutorial for all users, teachers, and parents

Materials Needed

Before you begin, make sure you have the following items ready to use with this book.

- **a set of wooden or plastic alphabet letters**
- **sharp pencil**
- **tape recorder**
- **blank tape**
  student's practice tape
- **a set of crayons**
- **ruler**
- **scissors**
- **Reading and Spelling Pack Cards**
  Photocopy pages 137 to 148 from the book. Each student will need a set of cards.
- **an exercise book**
  Photocopy lined paper, page 27.

In addition to these materials, you may like to try using the following:

- **pencil grip**
- **blackboard (and chalk) or sand-tray**
  Use for tracing letter shapes with chalk or finger-tracking. (Large sheets of scrap paper such as newsprint and thick felt pens can be used for the same purpose.)
- **egg timer or stopwatch**

Introduction
Tutorial for all users, teachers, and parents

This section of our book has been designed to show you, the parent or teacher of a non-reading child, how to help your student get the best out of this book.

All of the necessary instructions are on the exercise pages. Before you get started, however, we suggest you read through these guidelines to enable you to use the material effectively.

Having worked through *Books 1* and *2*, you should have most of the necessary materials mentioned on page 8.

In addition, for this book, you will need a set of lowercase wooden or plastic letters.

If you have not completed *Books 1* and *2* you will soon be aware of whether your student is ready for *Book 3* after s/he has completed the tests on pages 30 and 31. It is vital that any gaps in your student's phonic knowledge be dealt with before starting this book.

You should also be aware that your student will have missed out on the basic teaching of:
- Handwriting and/or prewriting skills
- Sequencing of the alphabet
- Techniques of: "Read, Record, Listen, Repeat, Spell, Write"
    - Working with sound pictures
    - Working with word families and rhyming
- Instant words
- Identifying consonants and vowels and using these skills for splitting words into syllables
- Essential spellings
- Practicing two and three letter consonant blends
- Introduction to nouns and verbs

The authors have found that it often pays to begin at the beginning. When trying to slot students into the system who already have some phonic skill, it is frequently necessary to backtrack to ensure that all the links are established between the alphabetic name of letter, the sound of letter, the recognition of letter symbol, and the ability to write the letter neatly.

If you are ready to begin *Book 3* with your student, having completed *Books 1* and *2*, we suggest that you read through the teacher's notes to remind yourself of the main teaching points before you begin working with your student on this book.

You will notice that every time a letter is introduced, a similar format is followed. Open the book to Page 58 and we will take you through the format for van **v** using the following instructions in this section.

1. Alphabet Arc

It will be helpful if you can obtain a set of wooden alphabet letters, both capital and lowercase *(see Materials Needed, page 8).*

CAPITAL LETTERS are used at first, because they are easier to distinguish than the lowercase letters. You will notice, however, that on page 114 we introduce the lowercase letters. If your student is able to sequence the uppercase letters with no difficulty and consistently sets them out in the correct orientation (for example, facing the correct way, not back-to-front or upside down), then s/he will be ready to progress to the lowercase letters. If s/he is still experiencing difficulty with uppercase letters, do not confuse the issue by introducing lowercase letters until s/he is ready for this stage. Some students will not be ready for this until the beginning of *Book 4* in the series.

Figure 1

You will have to help your student/s to do this in the early stages. Have them put the letters **A, MN,** and **Z** in place first, to form a framework. As they do so, have them they say:

"A on the left, Z on the right, and M and N in the middle."

Each time you do this in the daily lesson have your students repeat this formula.

They must now complete the arc of the alphabet working from left to right.

Absolute beginners may need an aid. Make four cards, as follows:

1) **A B C D**   2) **E F G H I J K L M**
3) **N O P Q R**   4) **S T U V W X Y Z**

Allow the students to tear up each card as soon as it is no longer needed. This will give them great satisfaction!

You will notice that the alphabet arc is not appearing quite as frequently now as it did in *Books 1* and *2*. It is still just as important that this is a part of every daily lesson until your student is totally familiar with the sequencing (where the letters are positioned) and orientation (which way the letters face) in the arc. You should be using this opportunity to review any words your student is having difficulty spelling or reading, as well as using the time to drill new letters or combinations of letters as they occur in the book. Remember, however, not to expect your student to read or spell any word containing letters which have not yet been taught.

Together you can have fun making up little gimmicks as reminders.

Examples:
> **"J and K are always back-to-back."**
> **"N should be like the first half of M."**
> (You can show your students by having them put it on top to see if it matches.)
> **"The line stroke on Q should be pointing the way we are going—towards Z"** . . . and so on.

When you are both happy that the alphabet arc is correctly sequenced, you can play games as follows:

1) Student shuts his/her eyes, you remove a letter, and close up the space.
   Student opens his/her eyes and tells you which letter has disappeared.
   Student then replaces the letter correctly.
   This game is useful for reinforcing names or shapes of letters which pose a problem.

2) Student shuts his/her eyes and picks out a letter at random. Can s/he tell you its name just by feeling its shape? If this is difficult for the student, stick to letters which have already been introduced in the book.

3) Student shuts his/her eyes while you exchange two letters in the arc. Student opens his/her eyes and discovers which letters are out of sequence.

4) Take turns saying the sequence of the alphabet from A to Z, for example, naming one letter each. Next increase to two letters, then three, and so on.

5) As your student becomes more able, s/he can be timed putting out the alphabet arc using an egg timer or a stopwatch and trying to beat the previous time. Keep a record of the time taken. It can be very motivating. When putting the letters away, call a sequence of letters at random. Have your student put them in the same order in front of her/him and then put them in the box, in that order, saying the letter names as this is done. As soon as the student is confident with three letters, increase the squence to four, and so on. This will help to improve his/her listening memory, attention span, and familiarity with the ordering of the alphabet.

2. Auditory and Visual Introductions

For best learning results students must become active learners. When a new letter or concept is first introduced it is vital to have your students' full attention. I think one gets the best results when new introductions are made with direct instruction and some active discovery on the students' part. The introductions should also be somewhat consistent. This population of learners feels more secure when there is some consistency. When a new letter or concept is first introduced, there needs to be much teacher/tutor involvement.

Procedure: **Auditory Introduction**
Student needs to be reminded to: Listen, Repeat, Discover, and Answer

Teacher says, "I will give you a list of words; you need to listen carefully to each word. Repeat each word after me. Try to discover what sounds are alike in each word."

bat, bid, band, sob, tab

Teacher says, "What sound was the same in each of these words?" If the student is not able to answer, then repeat the process again. This time accent the letter/sound you are trying to introduce.

Procedure: **Visual Introduction**
Student needs to be reminded to: Listen and Watch carefully

1) Teacher writes the words on the board. These are the same words used for the auditory introduction. The teacher says each sound as s/he writes the corresponding letter. Make sure you have your students' attention.

2) Ask students to watch as you point to each letter and sound out the word.

3) Ask your students what *letter or letters* make the sound you just introduced in the auditory introduction.

Word list for auditory and visual introductions

Introduction letters ng:	sing, long, clang, rang, bring, strong
Introduction letters th:	thin, that, them, cloth, bath, with
Introduction letters ck:	block, lick, tack, neck, buck, stack
Introduction letter v:	vast, vent, van, vest, vet
Introduction letter w:	wax, win, well, with, wink
Introduction letter j:	just, jump, jam, jet, job
Introduction letter y:	yell, yes, yap, yank, yo-yo
Introduction letters sh:	shot, shut, she, ship, dash, fish, mesh
Introduction letters qu:	quick, quit, quilt, quell, quill, quack
Introduction letter x:	box, fox, ax, tax, Rex, wax, fix
Introduction letter z:	zip, zig, zag, zap, zest, fuzz, buzz
Introduction letters ff:	cuff, sniff, puff, snuff, staff, scoff
Introduction letters ch:	chimp, check, chip, champ, chill, ranch, much

3. Listen to the Teacher Section

Simply read the words, steadily and clearly to the student, giving him/her plenty of time to consider whether the sound listened for has been heard.

Transcript for the Auditory Exercises Which Accompany Book 3

The teacher reads this section of the lesson to the child. For independent students, the teacher may wish to tape record this section for the student.

Page 32, Section 6: Write **ng** in the box if you hear **ng** in the word.
   1. sing   2. gang   3. fox   4. string   5. hung   6. black   7. king   8. air

Page 34, Section 1: Write the words you hear under the correct heading **ng** **ng** or **nk** **nk**.
   1. sang   2. rink   3. sting   4. hunk   5. king   6. brink   7. sank   8. ring   9. stink
   10. hung   11. kink   12. bring   13. string   14. plank   15. rang   16. skunk

Page 36, Section 1: Listen to these sentences and fill in the missing words.
   1. The raft sinks to the sand bank.   2. Can you mend the tent?
   3. The ant ran along his hand.   4. He flung himself on the bunk.
   5. I think it is spring. Here are the plants.

Page 39, Section 6: Write **th** in the box if you hear **th** in the word.
   1. then   2. path   3. thank   4. friend   5. cloth   6. frill   7. depth   8. thug

Page 41, Section 2: Write the words under the correct heading **f** or **th**.
   1. fin   2. that   3. fat   4. thin   5. thus   6. fuss   7. fan   8. thank

Page 43, Section 1: Listen to these words and sentences and write **th** or **f** to complete each word.
   1. them   2. bath   3. fall   4. fact   5. think   6. this   7. thing   8. fell   9. fist   10. fuss
   1. This cloth is not as thin as that cloth.   2. Did Ted's fist thump that man?
   3. That froth slips past the plug fast.
   4. The plinth at the bottom of that pillar strengthens it and stops it from falling.

Page 47, Section 1: Write **ck** in the middle box if you hear the **k** sound in the middle of the word or in the end box if you hear the **k** sound at the end of the word.
   1. back   2. stuck   3. pocket   4. ticket   5. deck   6. block   7. flick   8. cricket

Page 49, Section 1: Listen to these words. You must think about which vowel sound you hear before the **k** ck in each word. Then write the word in the correct column according to that vowel.
   1. thick   2. back   3. stock   4. speck   5. pluck   6. struck   7. deck
   8. block   9. trick   10. black   11. stack   12. suck   13. click   14. frock
   15. fleck   16. buck   17. pick   18. smack

© LDA   13   LL80103 *Reading Success Book 3*

Page 50, Section 2: Write the words in the correct column, **-ck -nk -lk**.
    1. silk 2. think 3. track 4. milk 5. dock 6. link 7. hulk 8. bank
    9. peck 10. flick 11. sulk 12. trunk

Page 59, Section 1: Write **v** in the box if you hear **v** in the word.
    1. village 2. fog 3. give 4. vacuum 5. liver 6. than 7. valley 8. rave

Page 62, Section 1: Write **w** in the box if you hear **w** in the word.
    1. wing 2. wood 3. with 4. wig 5. worm 6. lip 7. sandwich 8. pin

Page 63, Section 1: Listen and fill in **sw** or **tw**.
    1. swing 2. twist 3. swap 4. swill 5. swam 6. twigs 7. swell 8. twins
    9. twang 10. twill 11. swift 12. swept

Page 67, Section 2: SPELLING TEST
    1. tank 2. strong 3. ink 4. long 5. contest 6. thug 7. think 8. bath
    9. her 10. could 11. these 12. come 13. sending 14. black 15. stick
    16. taken 17. begin 18. vast 19. went 20. about

Page 69, Section 1: Write **j** in the box if you hear **j** in the word.
    1. June 2. shoe 3. jump 4. tune 5. Jamaica 6. cherry 7. judge 8. job

Page 73, Section 1: Write **y** in the box if you hear **y** in the word.
    1. yellow 2. ward 3. yard 4. yank 5. shop 6. yes 7. canyon 8. yodel

Page 75, Section 2: Write these words in the correct column according to the vowel sound you hear in the first syllable.
    1. publish 2. robot 3. magnet 4. wigwam 5. tulip 6. pilot
    7. rocket 8. taken

Page 77, Section 7: Write **sh** in the box if you hear **sh** in the word.
    1. shop 2. chip 3. brush 4. fishing 5. sock 6. shine 7. polish 8. bishop

Page 83: On this page you are going to design 6 flags. Make sure you have a pencil, a ruler, and some colored pencils before you begin. Now listen carefully to all the instructions for each flag design before you do anything. Divide the first flag into three equal parts by drawing two lines from left to right. These are called horizontal lines. Now color the middle section blue. Look at the second flag. Draw a line from the top left-hand corner to the bottom right-hand corner. Now draw another line from the top right-hand corner to the bottom left-hand corner. These are called diagonal lines. You will now have four triangles. Color the bottom triangle green. On the third flag draw one line across the top left-hand corner. Now draw another line across the bottom right-hand corner, making a triangle at each corner. Color the top left-hand triangle red. In the center of the fourth flag, draw the largest circle you can. The circle must fill the center of the flag. Write N for north, S for south, E for east, and W for west where the circle touches the edges of the flag. Check that you have placed these compass points in the correct positions. Pattern the circle in any way you choose. Divide the fifth flag into 3 equal sections by drawing two lines from top to bottom. We call these vertical lines. Color the right-hand section yellow. Draw a horizontal line from from left to right to divide the sixth flag in half. Now draw a vertical line from top to bottom to divide the flag into four equal quarters. These are called rectangles. Color the rectangle on the bottom left-hand side brown.

Page 94, Section 1: Write **qu** in the box if you hear a **kw** sound in the word.
1. kick 2. queen 3. quarter 4. quilt 5. request 6. squid 7. keen 8. quite

Page 99, Section 1: Write **x** in the box if you hear **k s** in the word.
1. fox 2. pass 3. index 4. mix 5. relax 6. lack 7. expect 8. expand

Page 110, Section 1: Write **z** in the box if you hear **z** in the word.
1. zebra 2. zany 3. zip 4. sip 5. fizzy 6. Zambia 7. lazy 8. rave

Page 112, Section 3: SPELLING TEST
1. jumping 2. yank 3. what 4. broken 5. shock 6. thrush 7. wasp
8. because 9. any 10. quick 11. shopping 12. next 13. asked 14. zip
15. have 16. were 17. jacket 18. yes 19. tulip 20. crash

Page 116, Section 7: Write **ff** in the box if the one beat word ends in **f**.
1. give 2. stiff 3. cuff 4. path 5. lift 6. puff 7. staff 8. quaff

Page 126, Section 1: Write **ch** in the box if your hear **ch** in the word.
1. choose 2. hutch 3. brash 4. chicken 5. cherish 6. wish
7. witch 8. China

4. Reading Pack and Sound Picture/Spelling Pack

The set of cards for reading and spelling at the back of this book covers only those letters introduced in *Book 3*.

Notice that the new cards are introduced at this level to include the spelling choices **d** and **t**. Refer to pages 147 and 148. A Sound Picture/Spelling Pack Card has not been included since this is a regular suffix ending covered by the cards **e** and **d**. Example: **ed**.

In *Book 1* you will have had the Reading Pack Cards:
n   c   d   p   t   r   s   cr   dr   pr   tr   str   scr   spr   st   sp

the Sound Picture/Spelling Pack Cards: p   k   d   n   r   s   t

and the long and short vowels: a   e   i   o   u

In *Book 2* you will have had the long and short vowels: a   e   i   o   u

the Reading Pack Cards:
m   mp   h   nd   nt   b   br   l   sl   pl   cl   bl   -ll   -ss   f   fr

and the Sound Picture/Spelling Pack Cards:
fl   g   gl   gr   k   sk   m   h   b   l   s   f   g   k

After completing *Book 1* and *Book 2*, your student should be coping confidently with a sequence of four letters. Increase this to five letters as soon as four is being managed consistently. It helps to have a competition here. If the student gets the sequence and the names of letters correct, s/he earns one point. If not, you get the point. The student tries to beat you by scoring more points. If s/he wins easily, you could try incorporating an extra letter in the sequence to be remembered.

Your student should now be gaining in confidence, increasing his/her attention span, and improving his/her auditory memory. Alphabet letters should continue to be used to reinforce spelling patterns. This is a structured course. Words for spelling must contain only the letters already covered. For example, **sw** and **tw** may be used only when the student has progressed beyond page 63. If your student is asked to spell the word "swim" and produces "sim" with the wooden letters you must then ask your student to read the word, helping him/her to see that it says "sim" and not "swim." You then need to ask "What do we need to add to change the word from sim to swim?"

Get your student to feel the sound with the teeth, lips, and tongue as s/he practices making the **sw** sound. When the letters have been replaced in the arc, ask her/him to make **swam, swank, swill,** etc. until the sw blend has become established. Any sound presenting difficulty needs to be drilled daily until the student produces an automatically correct response. Another fun activity using the wooden alphabet letters is to have your student make the word "swimming." Ask "How many words can you make using the letters from this two-syllable word?" You should find at least 10. Remember the alphabet is a considerable hurdle on the route to literacy and has to be something your student is able to cope with confidently.

Sound Picture/Spelling Pack
This is your HEARING and WRITING Pack.

On the FRONT of the card is the Sound Picture, which is a white letter in a black pentagon. It is a symbol representing the sound to be said instead of the letter's name. It is designed to aid orientation and indicates the left/right direction needed for reading and spelling.

For example, the Sound Picture **v** should be said "vuh" and not "vee."

On the BACK of the card is the information that the student needs to complete the associations relevant to that particular sound.

TOP LEFT The Sound Picture (see Figure 2, below).
(you will notice that the sounds **ng**, **th**, **ch**, and **sh** have a white line underneath which is to indicate that the two letters represent one sound)

Immediately below this you will see the blank handwriting format. This is to enable the teacher to write the relevant form of the letter (uppercase or lowercase) or the spelling choice, where more than one exists (example: **c, k, ck**). This is designed to reinforce the concept of choice in the spelling of sounds. Refer to the example for sound picture exercises in Figure 5, page 18.

If the cards have been laminated, the relevant spelling choice should be written on the handwritten format using a water-based felt pen. This can then be wiped off and changed as necessary. If laminated cards are not used, then new cards can be issued at any time and changed as needed.

TOP RIGHT This is the Clueword Picture.
Below this is the example of the handwritten form of the letter on the handwriting format with the second spelling choice where applicable.

BOTTOM RIGHT An example of the handwritten form of the capital letter.

To use the Sound Picture/Spelling Pack, tell the student "This is your HEARING and WRITING Pack. It tells you which sound to say with your mouth and also which sound to listen for with your ears."

Figure 2

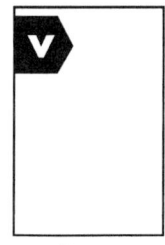
Front

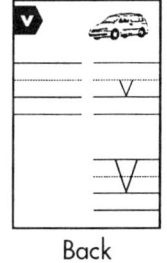
Back

1. The student must have the Sound Picture side (FRONT) of the card facing him/her. for example, **v**.

   Looking at this, the student must say the sound "vuh" and then name the letter "vee."

2. Then the letter must be written on a copy of the lined Practice Sheet.

3. When the letter has been written, the student turns over the card and compares his/her handwriting with the example. If incorrect, as in the Reading Pack, it goes to the bottom of the pack for a second try. At first you may need to practice this routine with your student, but eventually s/he should be able to do this task independently.

The Sound Picture/Spelling Pack should be used to help with the Sound Pictures word exercises. At this stage, these exercises have been extended to include spelling choices. Draw your student's attention to the fact that the spelling choice should be written under the Sound Picture on the format provided, before starting to use the card (see Figure 3 below). These may need to be changed when an alternative choice is required. Hence the importance of using a water-based pen.

For example, line up the Sound Pictures on the back of the Spelling Pack by overlapping successive cards, working left to right (see Figure 4). Spelling is given by the written letters below the sound pictures.

Sometimes a Sound Picture is different from the letter that you write. For example, the Sound Picture **k** can be written as **c, k,** or **ck**. The **ck** spelling is introduced on page 46 in this book. Prior to this page in the book the response to the sound picture **k** will be to write the letter **c** or **k**. Subsequent to this page, however, the response to the Sound Picture **k** will be **c, k,** or **ck**.

Figure 3

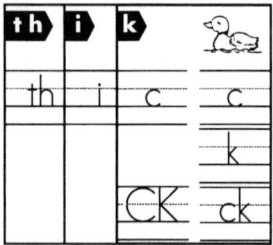

The student selects the required spelling choice and writes it under the Sound Picture using a water-based pen.

Students were introduced to long vowel sounds in *Book 2*. They now have the opportunity to work with open syllables and long vowel sounds in longer words. Long vowel sounds are double the length of short ones and use alphabetic letter names and uppercase letter forms to emphasize the long sounds (see Figure 4 below).

Figure 4

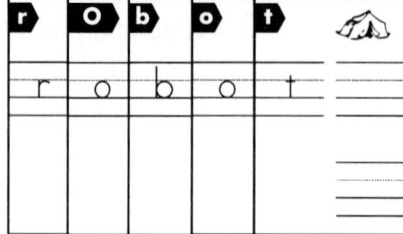

Games can also be played with the Sound Picture/Spelling Pack. For example:

1) SNAP   Add additional cards to ensure that there are enough duplicates. Shout out the sound of the card, instead of "snap," to win the cards in the pile.

2) I SPY   Can be played using the sounds on the cards in the normal way. This challenges the players to think of other words having the same sound.

5. Instant Words

We have introduced more of these words which do not necessarily follow the structured teaching in this program but, because they occur frequently in all reading material, we feel your students will need to be able to recognize them INSTANTLY on sight (LOOK and SAY). Your student will not necessarily be expected to be able to spell these words at this stage.

6. Reading Games For Instant Words
(or other difficult words)

Write each word on 4 cards. For example, a group of 10 words would make a pack of 40 cards. These cards can then be used for traditional games of: SNAP, RUMMY, PELMANISM (PAIRS), HAPPY FAMILIES, or simply for sorting.

The word should be read every time it is picked up.

The cards may also be used with board games, or any game involving the throwing of dice.

FAMILY FOURS can be played with a minimum of 3 players. The stack of cards is placed facedown in the middle of the table and each player in turn, picks up a card and reads it. The card is then placed faceup in front of the player. The next player reads his/her card and checks whether there are any matching cards in front of any other player. If s/he spots one, s/he is entitled to ask the player for this card which is then placed in her/his pack. In this way, s/he begins to build up "families" of four matching cards. The winner is the player who collects the most families. Margaret Combley taught us this game.

In this book on page 43, Section 3 there is an opportunity to play a memory game. If your student has a severe problem with recall, you will first need to play this game with actual items put out on a tray. Start with five or six dissimilar items. Allow your student one minute to memorize these, then cover the tray and see if the items can be remembered. Gradually increase the number of items on the tray.

Page 35—Glue the photocopied sheet onto cardstock and cover with clear adhesive paper or laminate. Then have your student cut up the photocopied sheet and mix up the cards. See if your student can place the shuffled cards in the same order as on the original page. Compare results, and if unsuccessful, try again in subsequent lessons. Alternatively, use this page, photocopied several times, for playing PELMANISM (PAIRS). This page can also be used to stimulate your student's ability to invent situations. Select one or two cards at random and connect them in some way to make a story. S/he will probably need an example for help in the beginning before s/he is able to do this independently.

Page 49—Here is an opportunity to play Rhyming I Spy, for example, "I spy . . . something that rhymes with 'clock.'" (The player must write down the word s/he has chosen, for example, "flock.") If another player answers "sock" this might be correct as a rhyming word, but not the one that was written down. In a small group situation, score points as follows: 1 point for a rhyming word and 2 points for the correct rhyme. It would be necessary to take turns.

Page 53—Stubby's hockey game
This basic board game may be used for learning difficult words. You will need to change the word walls to the relevant problem words. Give the student a sticker or a small treat as a reward at the end of the game.

Page 67—It sometimes helps to teach the correct spelling of "there" to say that "there's got a 'here.'"

Page 90—To teach "because," say "big elephants can't always use small exits."

Pages 123–124—Stubby's cross country run
This can be played as a reading game where the student has to throw a die and read the notices before going on. It can also be used to teach or test the controlled vocabulary at any stage of the course. You will need to make suitable packs of cards for this purpose with numbers corresponding to those on the track on one side and a sentence to be read or a word to be spelled on the other side.

More fun activities for alphabet work and for using the Reading Pack and Sound Picture/Spelling Pack Cards are covered under Sections 1 and 4 of this tutorial.

Your bright pupils will have fun making up their own mnemonics for difficult spelling patterns.

Remember that limericks, jokes, and humorous verse are valuable aids in the teaching of reading and comprehension.

7. Controlled Vocabulary

Reading and Spelling passages throughout the book are carefully structured to contain only letters that have been taught. Students are never asked to read (with the exception of INSTANT WORDS) or write letters which have not been covered in the structure. This builds confidence and a feeling of success.

8. Word Families and Rhyming

Considerable emphasis has been placed on rhyming in this book. This is intended as a spelling aid and not an introduction to poetry.

9. Grammar

Basic elements of grammar have been introduced throughout the series. See the Table of Contents, pages 4–6.

10. Irlen Syndrome
(Scotopic Sensitivity Syndrome)

Since many children have difficulty with black print on white paper, we suggest that teachers experiment using various pastel shades of paper when photocopying. This will establish which color is most helpful in reducing the glare and distortion which may be experienced by children suffering from Scotopic Sensitivity Syndrome (Irlen Syndrome).

If the student is helped by the colored paper, try using colored overlays on top of reading material.

11. Record Page

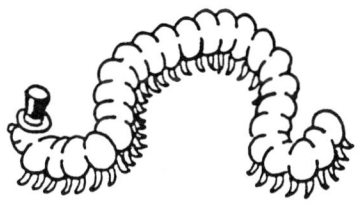

The Caterpillar Logo reminds the student to fill in the letter on the Record Page, found on page 22, when s/he has completed the required work for that letter. The student simply finds the segment with the letter s/he has just learned and traces over it. By the time s/he has completed *Books 1, 2,* and *3,* the caterpillar will be complete.

Make sure your student knows the sound, name, and written shape of the letter before allowing it to be filled in.

12. To Sum Up

Each daily lesson you and/or your students should
    Mark the previous day's worksheets
    Practice the Reading Pack
    Do the alphabet work
    Practice the Spelling Pack and spell words to reinforce work done with wooden letters
    Complete new sheets
    Play reading games
    Praise and/or reward the student when s/he has made a real effort

13. Conclusion

We hope that by this stage in the series your student is gaining in confidence and feels that s/he is able to read, write, and spell. We wish you well in your endeavors to help your student achieve success. Remember your emphasis should always be on positive reinforcement and praise.

Photocopy for each child using this program.

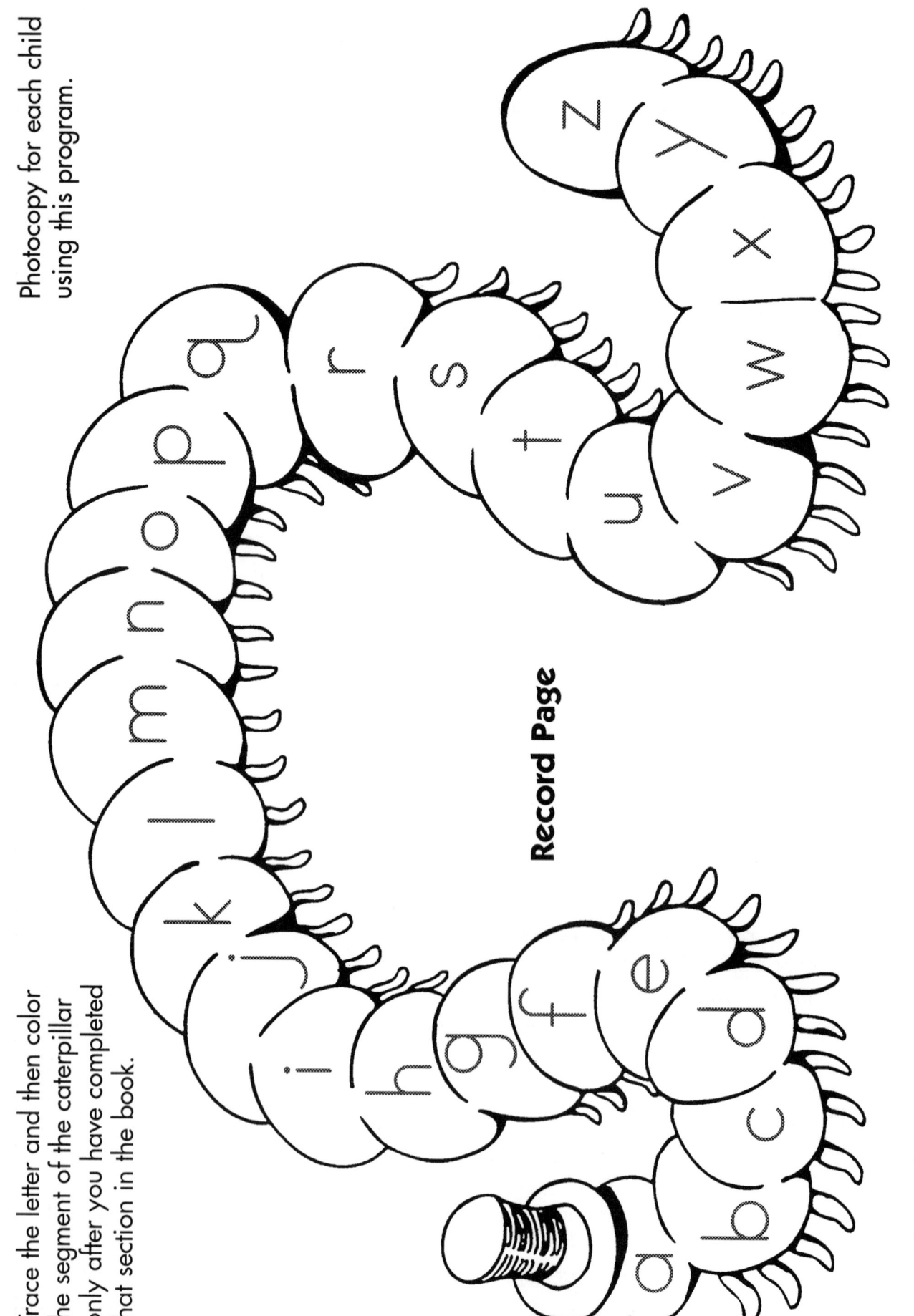

Record Page

Trace the letter and then color the segment of the caterpillar only after you have completed that section in the book.

Glue to the top of a file folder. Children can keep papers in the folder and color the incentive caterpillar.

© LDA

LL80103 *Reading Success Book 3*

Manuscript Uppercase Chart

A B C D

E F G H

I J K L

M N O P

Q R S T

U V W X

Y Z

Manuscript Lowercase Chart

a b c d

e f g h

i j k l

m n o p

q r s t

u v w x

y z

Cursive Uppercase Chart

A	*B*	*C*	*D*
E	*F*	*G*	*H*
I	*J*	*K*	*L*
M	*N*	*O*	*P*
Q	*R*	*S*	*T*
U	*V*	*W*	*X*
Y	*Z*		

Cursive Lowercase Chart

a b c d

e f g h

i j k l

m n o p

q r s t

u v w x

y z

Handwriting Practice

The Lessons

What do you remember from *Book 1* and *Book 2*?

1. Write the letter or letters for each Sound Picture.

t _____

i _____

p _____

n _____

s _____
1) _____ 2) _____

a _____

d _____

k _____
1) _____ 2) _____

o _____

r _____

m _____

e _____

h _____

b _____

l _____
1) _____ 2) _____

f _____

g _____

u _____

If you wrote the letters correctly you may fill in and color these segments on the caterpillar record page.

2. Write the first 2 letters for these pictures.

Finding out what you know

1. Write the words for these pictures.

2. Track the alphabet.

Complete the alphabet tracking by putting a circle around each of the remaining alphabet letters. Circle all 26 letters in alphabetical order. Use red for vowels and green for consonants.

ⓐ	n	m	k	o	l	p	u	h	n	ⓑ	v	f	d	ⓒ
s	d	h	i	j	e	g	l	n	p	f	k	g	m	u
d	h	q	b	i	t	g	y	j	f	a	u	r	l	k
m	o	l	r	c	s	e	m	n	b	q	v	d	o	f
u	p	b	o	h	t	w	j	q	k	e	r	n	s	i
o	g	e	f	k	l	t	b	z	u	w	c	t	r	c
g	v	s	u	g	l	b	e	a	i	d	n	x	w	q
v	s	x	t	d	y	h	m	j	c	z	k	a	f	l

Consonant digraph –NG –ng

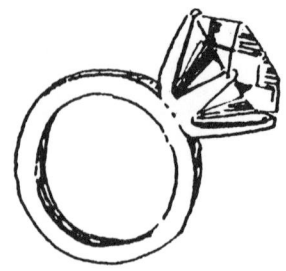

ring **ng**

1. Auditory Introduction. (See page 12.)
2. Visual Introduction. (See page 12.)
3. Introduce the clueword and Reading/Spelling Card.
4. Use the mirror and watch the mouth say **ng**. Say "ring". Air trapped behind the back of the tongue is released down the nose.
5. Write the letters on a board and talk about how each letter is formed. Have the student trace the letters at least three times.

6. Listen to the teacher. (See page 13.)
   Write **ng** in the box if you hear **ng** in the word.

1	2	3	4	5	6	7	8

7. Trace and copy in green, because **ng** is a consonant digraph.

ng ng ng

ring   spring

More about consonant digraph –NG –ng

1. Read the **-ng** and the **-nk** words.

sing	sting	string	rink	sink	stink
long	prong	strong	sank	plank	spank
gang	rang	sang	hung	king	kink

2. Trace the letters adding **-ng** to make a word. Then read the words.

ri___

si___　　　　　　　　　　　　　　　　　　　so___

stru___　　　　　　　　　　　　　　　　　stro___

lo___　　　　　　　　　　　　　　　　　　spra___

sprin___　　　　　　　　　　　flu___

pro___　　　　　bri___　　　　sla___

ru___　　　　　　cla___

3. Highlight the **-ng** and the **-nk** words in these sentences and read.

1. The truck made lots of smog.

2. Bud flung the plank and swung the trunk.

3. We had big chunks of ham and drank pink punch.

4. The insect stung my hand.

5. Ken has a mink and a skunk as pets.

6. The kids will get a swing set.

More about consonant digraph –NG –ng

1. Listen to the teacher. (See page 13.) Write the words your teacher gives you under the correct heading.

ng    **nk**

1.	9.
2.	10.
3.	11.
4.	12.
5.	13.
6.	14.
7.	15.
8.	16.

2. Now choose three words from Section 1 and use them in three good sentences. Write them in your exercise book. Remember that a sentence starts with a capital letter and ends with a period or a question mark.

3. Practice your reading and spelling cards.

Words ending in –nd –nt –nk –ng

Name the pictures. Write the words. Then play the games.

Now cut out the cards and use them to play Kim's game (memory training) or Pelmanism (pick up the pairs of words with the same endings). (See page 19.)

More –ng –nt –nd –nk endings

Complete the sentences.

1. Listen to the teacher. (See page 13.) Write the missing words in the spaces.

   1. The raft sinks to the _____ _____.
   2. Can you _____ the _____?
   3. The _____ ran along his _____.
   4. He _____ himself on the _____.
   5. I think it is _____. Here are the _____.

2. Use the pictures to help you complete these sentences.

   1. He _____ milk.
   2. It is _____. Send an S.O.S.
   3. She has lost a _____.
   4. The _____ belongs to the king.
   5. There is no _____ in the pen.

3. Word building with **i n k b r**. You try using **a n d l g**.

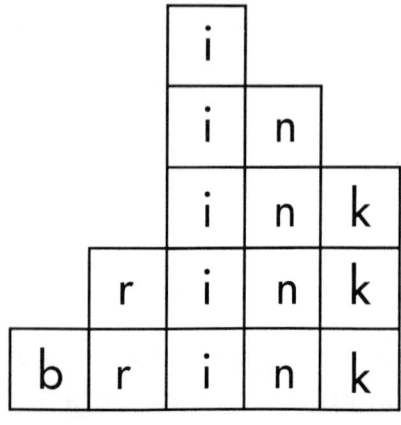
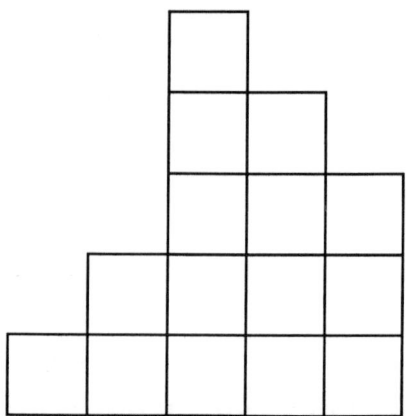

Puzzle words

1. Read.

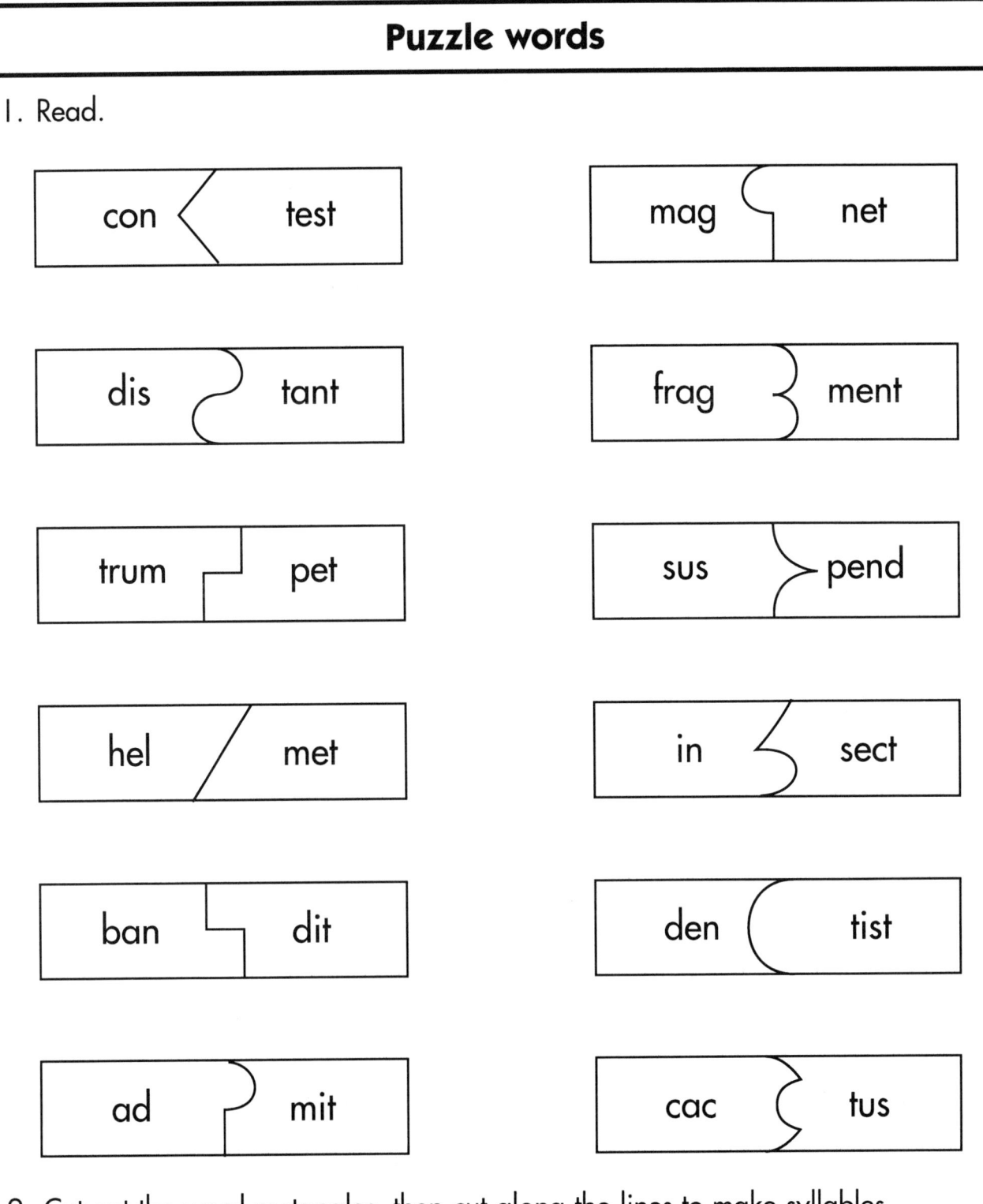

con — test	mag — net
dis — tant	frag — ment
trum — pet	sus — pend
hel — met	in — sect
ban — dit	den — tist
ad — mit	cac — tus

2. Cut out the word rectangles, then cut along the lines to make syllables.

3. How quickly can you fit the syllables together again to make words? Time yourself.

4. Dictation. Your teacher will give you some of the words from Section 1 on this page. Try to spell these words syllable-by-syllable. Write the words in your exercise book.

Alphabetical order
This helps you to use your dictionary.

*The letter **before b** is **a**.*
*The letter **after b** is **c**.*

1. Fill in the letters that come **before** these:

   ___n   ___d   ___m   ___f   ___i

   ___t   ___s   ___p   ___h   ___c

2. Fill in the letters that come **after** these:

   a___   k___   q___   d___   l___

   c___   r___   g___   t___   j___

3. Put these words in alphabetical order according to the first letter.

   goblin   **s**pring   **b**lanket   **t**ablet   **k**ing   **p**igment

Consonant digraph Th th

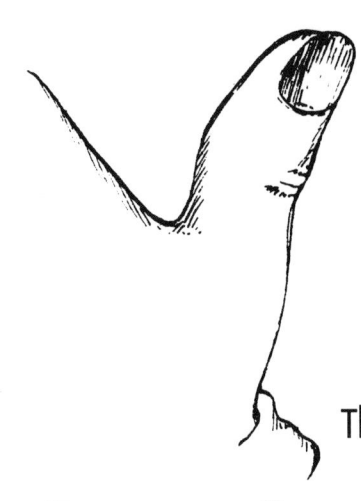

This is a **th**umb and that is a fea**th**er.

thumb th **feather** th

1. Auditory Introduction. (See page 12.)
2. Visual Introduction. (See page 12.)
3. Introduce the clueword and Reading/Spelling Card.
4. Use the mirror and watch the mouth say th. The tongue comes between upper and lower teeth and air is forced out between the tongue and upper teeth. Try saying th without voice and then with voice.
5. Write the letters on a board and talk about how each letter is formed. Have the student trace the letters at least three times.

6. Listen to the teacher. (See page 13.)
   Write **th** in the box if you hear a th in the word.

1	2	3	4	5	6	7	8

7. Trace and copy in green, because **th** serves as a consonant.

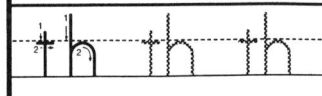

th th th

More about consonant digraph Th th

1. Read the **th** words.

thin	think	thank	path
this	that	them	then

2. Trace the letters adding **th** to make a word. Then read the words.

___ing   ba___ing   pa___   ba___tub

___en   ___an   ___ank   ___ick

wi___   clo___   fif___   ___is

3. Hear the difference between **th** and **f**.
Hold the mirror to your face and say the words **four** and **thumb**.
The sounds are close but your mouth and tongue change positions.
Say each word below as you look into the mirror.

f

fan	fist	fast	frog
flag	flop	frill	fell

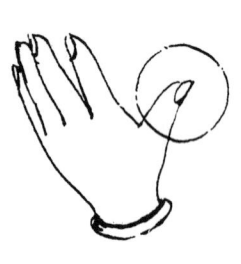

th

thin	think	thank	path
cloth	thug	thrill	bath

4. Write these words in your exercise book in alphabetical order. Look at the first letter and write the word in the same order as the alphabet.

depth   song   Athens

thing   cloth   froth

More about consonant digraph Th th

1. Circle the **th** words and read them to your teacher.

   There was a thin man from Hong Kong.

   His legs for the bath were too long.

   He sent for a cloth,

   Then got lost in the froth,

   And that is the end of this song, ding dong!

2. Listen to the teacher. (See page 13.) Write the words under the correct heading.

f	th

3. Practice your reading and spelling cards.
4. Dictation. Your teacher will give you some of the sentences in Section 1 for dictation. Write the dictation in your exercise book.

Essential Spellings

Work across ⟶

Read	Trace, naming letters	Write
1. that	that	
2. her	her	
3. for	for	
4. see	see	
5. these	these	
6. this	this	
7. then	then	
8. come	come	
9. there	there	
10. could	could	

More about th and f

1. Listen to the teacher (See page 13.) Trace the letters and write in the missing **th** or **f** to complete the words.

__em   ba__   __all   __act   __ink

__is   __ing   __ell   __ist   __uss

1. __is clo__ is not as __in as __at clo__.

2. Did Ted's __ist __ump __at man?

3. __at __roth slips past __e plug __ast.

4. __e plinth at __e bottom of __at pillar strengthens it and stops it __rom __alling.

2. Dictation. Your teacher will give you dictation using some of the sentences from Section 1 of this page. Write them in your exercise book.

3. Memory game. Name these pictures.
Look at them for 1 minute. Cover them and say how many you can remember.

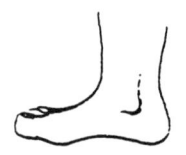

Instant words

1. Color the balloon when you have read the word.

   little · like · their · after · came · have

2. Read and use an arrowhead to choose the words which make good sense.

   Example:
   1. Dogs → (have) a strong instinct to smell things.
      — can sting you.
   2. Crabs / Frogs
      — like to run about on the sand.
   3. Hens
      — sit on their nests in spring.
      — can sing songs.
   4. Kittens / Rabbits
      — are little cats.
   5. Cats
      — like to run after rats.
      — can sit down on cactus plants.
   6. Pigs / Ants
      — came from little piglets.

3. Circle all the instant words you can find.
4. Copy the sentences in your exercise book. Remember punctuation.

Verbs and the ending –ing

A letter or group of letters added to the end of a word is call a **suffix**.

A verb is a doing (action) word. Every sentence **must have** a **verb** in order to make sense.
Sometimes the **suffix –ing** is added to a verb to suggest an action that is continuous or is still going on.

1. Read:

   rest ⟶ resting
   film ⟶ filming
   grill ⟶ grilling

2. Add **-ing** to the verb and use it to complete the sentence.

   1. melt

      The frost is _____.

   2. lift

      The strong man is _____ the trunk.

   3. think

      The lads are _____ about their trip.

   4. sing

      Pam is _____ a sad song.

   5. send

      Tom is _____ her a gift.

   6. miss

      Sam is _____ his dad.

Consonant digraph –CK –ck

ABCDEFGHIJKLMNOPQRSTUVWXYZ

duck k

1. Auditory Introduction. (See page 12.)
2. Visual Introduction. (See page 12.)
3. Introduce the clueword and Reading/Spelling Cards.
4. This comes at the end of a syllable (beat), after a short vowel sound.
5. Write the letters on a board and talk about how each letter is formed. Have students trace the letters at least three times.

6. Trace and copy in green, because **ck** serves as a consonant.

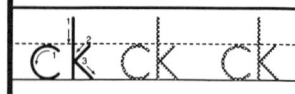

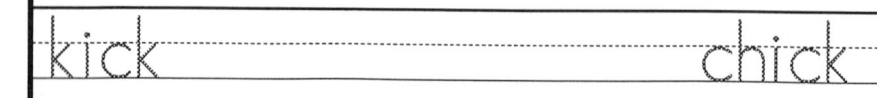

ck ck ck

kick   chick

© LDA   46   LL80103 *Reading Success Book 3*

More about consonant digraph –CK –ck

1. Listen to the teacher. (See page 13.) Write **ck** in the middle box if you hear the **k** sound in the middle of the word or the end box if you hear the sound at the end of the word.

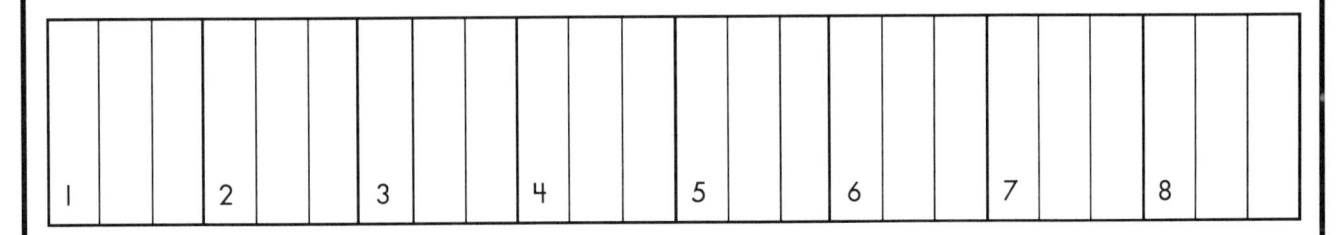

1	2	3	4	5	6	7	8

2. Code the vowels and read the words to your teacher. Notice that the **ck** is used when **k** follows **immediately** after a short vowel.

pick	pink	tank	tack	brick	brink
sank	sack	sick	silk	link	lick
buck	bunk	sunk	suck	stack	stank

3. Write **ck** under the picture if the **k** sound is at the end of the 1 beat (syllable) word.

4. Write **ck** under the picture where the **k** sound is in the middle of the word, at the end of the 1st beat (syllable).

More about consonant digraph –CK –ck

1. Highlight the **ck** words and read.

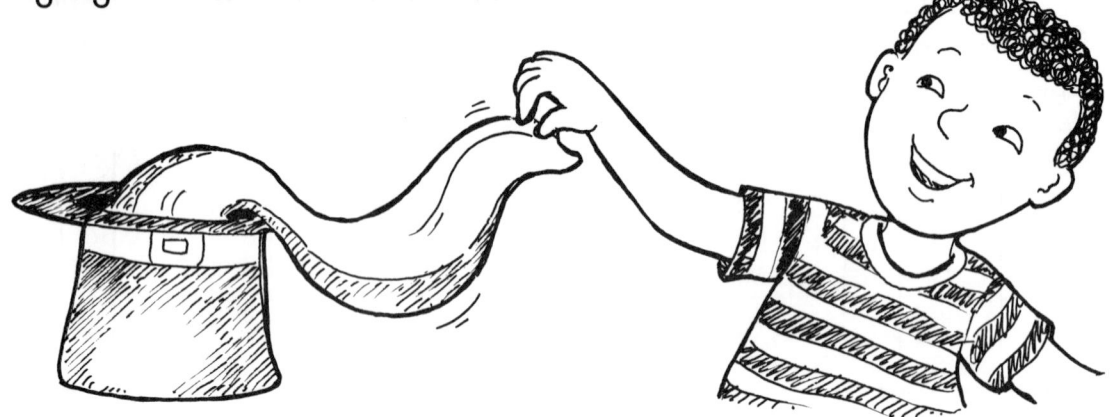

"I can do a slick trick," Sam tells Mick. He pulls a red silk ribbon from his pocket and snips it into ten strips. He tucks them into his top hat and taps it with his black stick.
"'Abra-ca-dabra!' Now pull the end of the ribbon," he instructs Mick. Mick grasps it and flicks it up. It's intact!

2. Trace the letters in the boxes and add **ck**, to make one syllable words. Mark the v c c pattern on each word and read the words to your teacher.

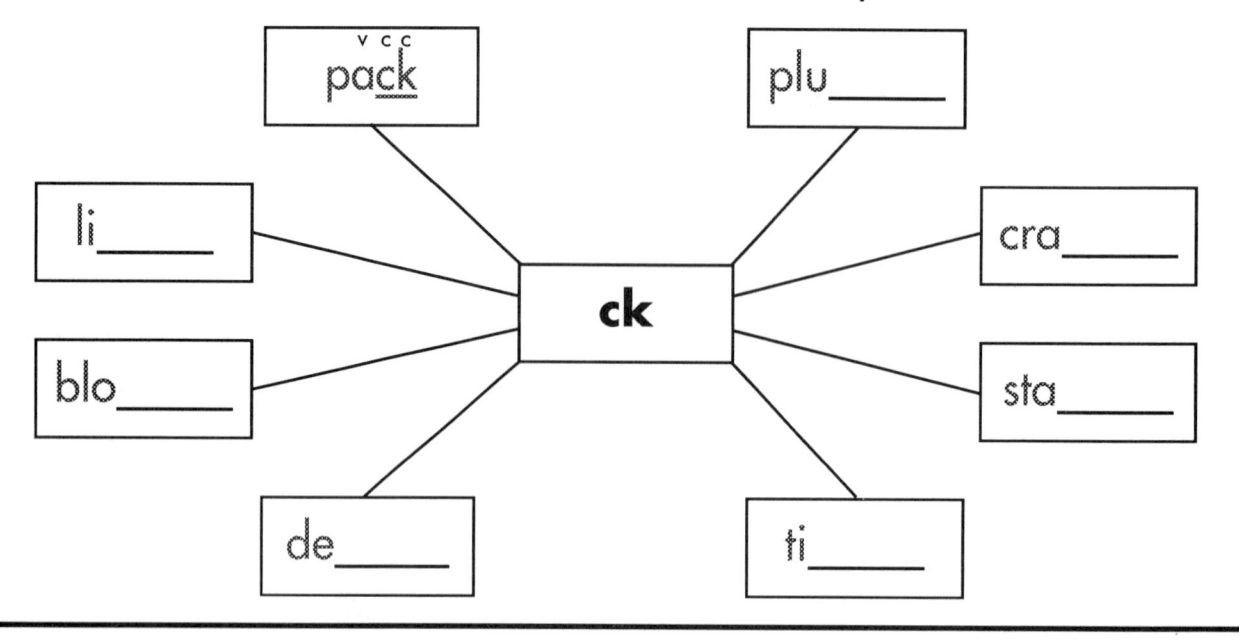

pack   plu____
li____   cra____
ck
blo____   sta____
de____   ti____

3. Practice your reading and spelling cards.
4. Dictation. Your teacher will give you some dictation from Section 1. Write the sentences in your exercise book.

Short vowels followed by –ck

1. Listen to the teacher. (See page 13.)

   Which vowel sound do you hear before **k** **ck** in each word?
   Write each word in the correct column.

i i	**a** a	**o** o	**e** e	**u** u

2. See if you can spell the names of these pictures.
   They all end with **ck**.

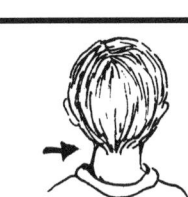

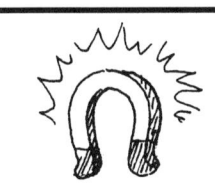

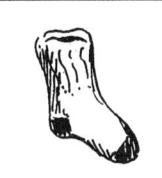

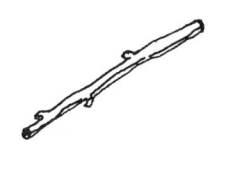

–ck or –k at the end of 1 syllable words

1. Read: A man had a spell of bad luck.
It began as he fell from his truck.
The truck ran downhill,
Struck a duck standing still,
Ran into the pond and got stuck!

2. Listen to the teacher. (See page 14.) Write the words in the correct column.

   Use **–ck** at the end of one syllable words, immediately after a short vowel.
   Examples: rack peck lick flock stuck
   Use **–k** after another consonant. Examples: sank elk mink honk bulk

   –ck   –nk   –lk

   _____   _____   _____

   _____   _____   _____

   _____   _____   _____

   _____   _____   _____

More about –ck or –k

1. Read these sentences. Trace the words and write in the correct endings in the blanks. They are all k sounds. You must work out how to spell them.

    1. The insect hid in a cra___ in the ban___.

    2. Pa___ Pam's sil___ fro___.

    3. Ni___ hit Ben in the ne___.

    4. Can he sin___ to the bottom of the tan___ and pi___ up the bri___?

    5. "Send him ba___ to the do___," said the man in bla___.

    6. Ted is fran___ about things.

2. Make up a sentence of your own for each of these words.
Write it in your exercise book.

    duck   luck   brick   rock   neck   black

3. Practice your reading and spelling cards.

    When you get to the k sound in your Spelling Pack you must now say the sound k and then tell yourself the alphabetical name choices, like this:

    k c   k k   k ck

    You must name and then write each of these 3 choices for the k sound.

Handwriting Practice
Trace and copy.

ng   thank

ring   ck

bring   sick

spring   brick

th   trick

thing

Nick props up the thick plank.

The stick insect clings to him.

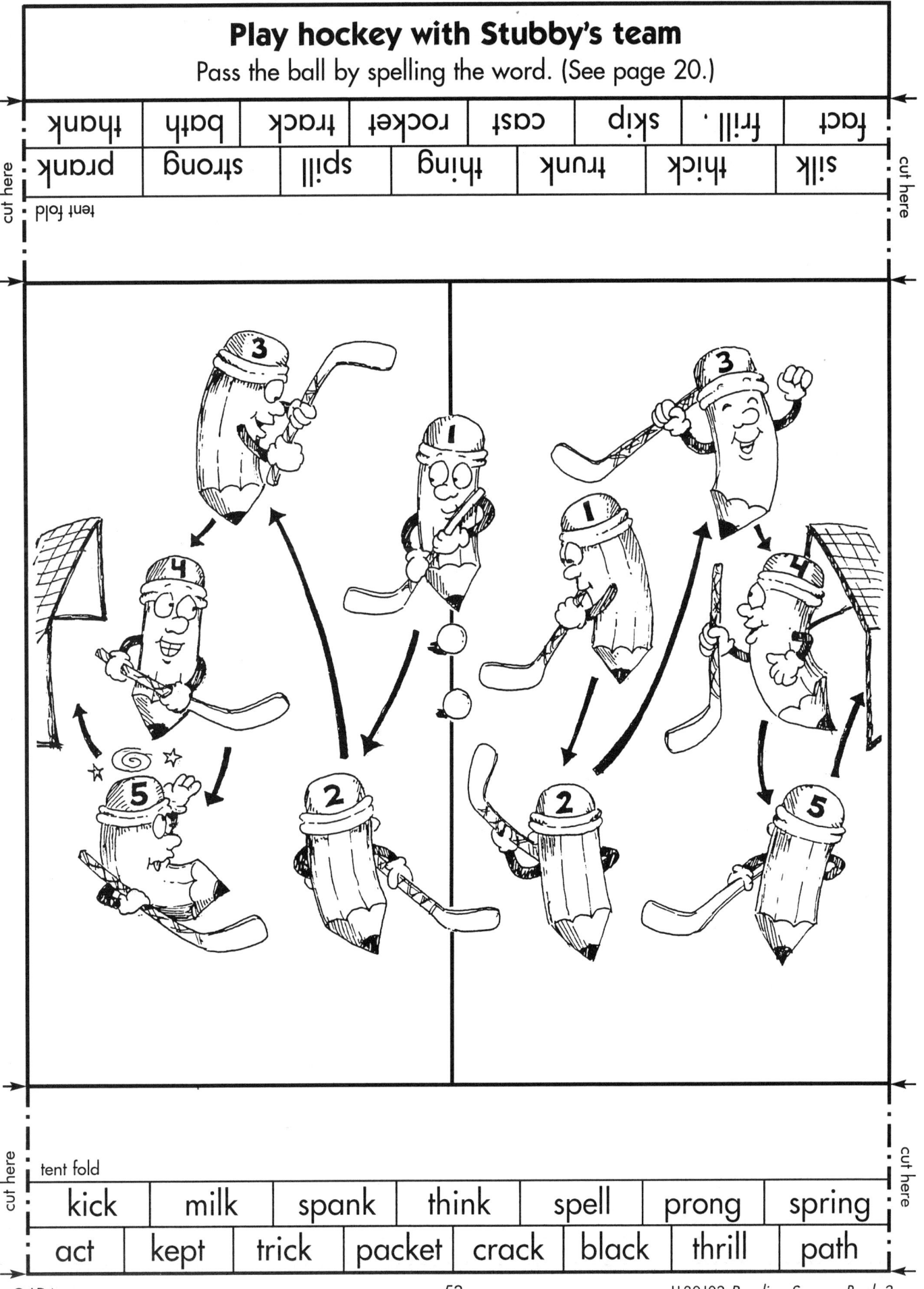

Play hockey with Stubby's team
Pass the ball by spelling the word. (See page 20.)

thank	bath	track	rocket	cast	skip	frill	fact
prank	strong	spill	thing	trunk	thick	silk	

kick	milk	spank	think	spell	prong	spring
act	kept	trick	packet	crack	black	thrill	path

Sound Pictures → Words

1. Use spelling pack cards to make these sound pictures.	2. Turn the cards over. Tell your hand what to write, naming the letters.	3. Write the word.
Look Say	Listen Name the letters (Tell your hand what to write.)	Write
1. th i k	-t-h-i-c-k-	1. thick
2. st i k		2.
3. k i k		3.
4. kr a k		4.
5. kl o k		5.
6. s i l k		6.
7. th a n k		7.

Syllables and vowel consonant patterns

ˇ short vowel ¯ long vowel

1. Do you remember?

one syllable

open
v̄
he

closed
v̌ c
hen

closed
v̌ c c
nest

v̄
be

v̌ c
Ben

v̌ c c
best

two syllables

closed   closed
v̌ c   c v̌
trum / pet

v̌ c   c v̌
ten / nis

2. Here is a new pattern.

Mark the v c pattern from the first vowel to the second vowel in each word.

1. basin   2. pilot   3. ripen   4. bacon

What pattern do you get? ☐

Correct answer: v c v

Rule: Split the v c v pattern like this: v / c v

3. Mark the v c pattern in these words. The first one has been done for you.

v̄ č v
tu/lip   ripen   crocus   silent

music   lupin   robot   begin

4. Split the above words into syllables.
5. Mark the vowels ¯ long or ˇ short.

See the next page.

V / V C pattern
Open and closed syllables

1. Here are the answers to Section 3 on page 55.

Open	Closed	Open	Closed	Open	Closed	Open	Closed
v̄	c v̆	v̄	c v̆	v̄	c v̆	v̄	c v̆
tu	lip	ri	pen	cro	cus	si	lent
v̄	c v̆	v̄	c v̆	v̄	c v̆	v̄	c v̆
mu	sic	lu	pin	ro	bot	be	gin

↑ Ends in a vowel   ↑ Ends in a consonant

2. a. Match the open and closed syllables to make words.

p I	pī	mŏn	m o n
b A	bā	kĕn	k e n
O	ō	lŏt	l o t
d E	dē	sĭn	s i n
r O	rō	pĕn	p e n
t A	tā	bŏt	b o t

b. Read the words.

Puzzle words

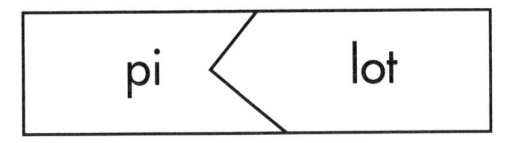

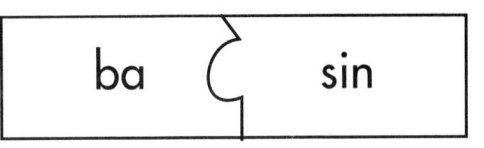

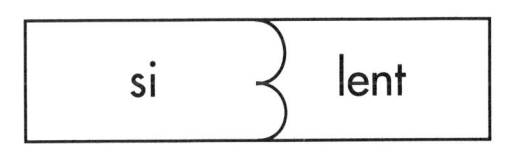

1. Read.

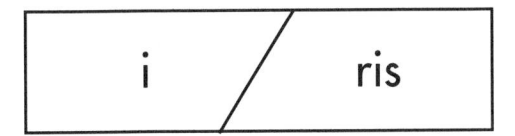

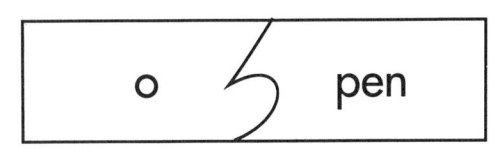

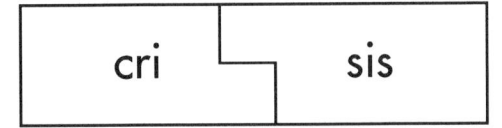

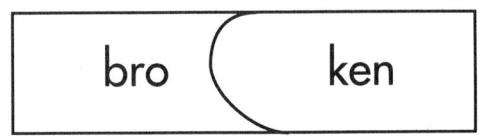

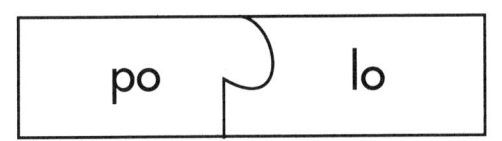

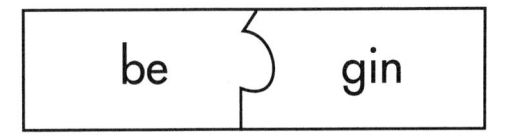

pi	lot	ba	sin
tu	lip	si	lent
cro	cus	de	mon
i	ris	o	pen
cri	sis	bro	ken
po	lo	be	gin

2. Cut out the word rectangles, then cut along the lines to make syllables.

3. How quickly can you fit the syllables together again to make words? Time yourself.

4. Dictation. Your teacher will give you some of the words from Section 1 on this page. Try to spell these words syllable-by-syllable. Write the words in your exercise book.

Letter V v — a consonant

ABCDEFGHIJKLMNOPQRSTUVWXYZ

van **v**

1. Make the alphabet arc.
2. Auditory Introduction. (See page 12.)
3. Visual Introduction. (See page 12.)
4. Introduce the clueword and Reading/Spelling Card.
5. Use the mirror and watch the mouth say **v**. Air is forced between the lower lip and the upper teeth as for **f** but with voicing.
6. Find the letter **V** in the alphabet arc. Feel its shape.
7. Write the letter on the board and talk about how the letter is formed. Have the student trace the letter at least three times.

8. Trace and copy in green, because **v** is a consonant.

V V V   v v v

vest   van

More about letter V v

1. Listen to the teacher. (See page 14.) Write **v** in the box if you hear **v** in the word.

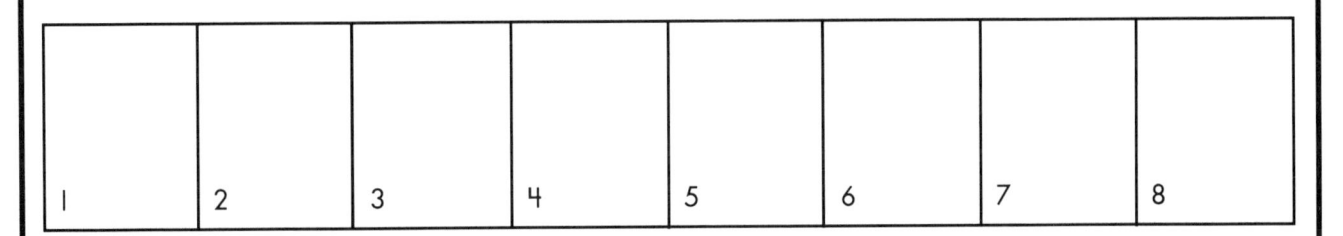

1	2	3	4	5	6	7	8

2. Fill in the missing letter with a **v** and then read the word.

____an   ____ast

    ____et   ____ent

       ____est   ____at

         ____im   ____andal

           ____iking

3. Mark the vccv or the vcv pattern, divide the syllables, code the vowels and read the word.

	vat	van	vamp
	vast	vend	veld
Example:	văn|dăl	velvet	victim
	vocal	vessel	Venus
	invest		viking

More about letter V v

1. In your dictionary find these words. Write the words and their definitions in your exercise book.

vellum	convulse
vagrant	vibrant
virus	veld

2. Copy the words from page 59, Section 3 under the correct headings.

vc/cv	v/cv	vc/cv/cv
1.		
2.		
3.		
4.		
5.		
6.		
7.		
8.		

3. Practice your reading and spelling cards.
4. Find and trace **v** on your caterpillar record page.

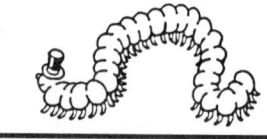

Letter W w — a consonant

ABCDEFGHIJKLMNOPQRSTUVWXYZ

windmill w

1. Make the alphabet arc.
2. Auditory Introduction. (See page 12.)
3. Visual Introduction. (See page 12.)
4. Introduce the clueword and Reading/Spelling Card.
5. Use the mirror and watch the mouth say w. w is made by pursing the lips in preparation for the vowel sound which follows it.
6. Find the letter **W** in the alphabet arc. Feel its shape.
7. Write the letter on the board and talk about how the letter is formed. Have the student trace the letter at least three times.

8. Trace and copy in green, because **w** is a consonant.

W W W   w w w

we   wing

More about letter W w

1. Listen to the teacher. (See page 14.) Write **w** in the box if you hear **w** in the word.

1	2	3	4	5	6	7	8

2. Read the **w** words to your teacher.

    with   will   win   wax   sandwich

3. Write **w** on the line if the picture begins with **w**.

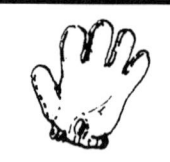

4. Write the letter **w** in the blanks and read.

  1. ____all   2. ____eb   3. ____ing   4. ____ill

  5. ____est   6. ____ag   7. ____ell   8. ____ith

  9. ____ink   10. ____ilt   11. ____ig____am

  12. ____ent   13. ____ind   14. ____edding

  15. ____illet   16. ____itness   17. ____ombat

5. Your teacher will give you some of the above words to finger spell in the sandtray.

More about letter W w

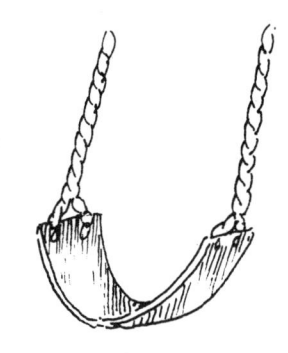

twins **tw** swing **sw**

Put the **tw**ins in the **sw**ings.

1. Listen as your teacher gives you some words. (See page 14.) Complete the words using **sw** or **tw**.

   1. _____ing   2. _____ist   3. _____ap

   4. _____ill   5. _____am   6. _____igs

   7. _____ell   8. _____ins   9. _____ang

   10. _____ill   11. _____ift 12. _____ept

2. Practice your reading and spelling cards.

   R S

3. Dictation. The teacher will read words from Section 1. Write them in your exercise book.

4. Find and trace **w** on your caterpillar record page.

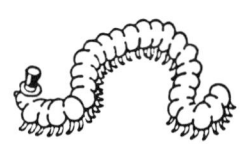

Handwriting Practice
Trace and copy.

v   va

ve   vim

Vin has a vast vest.

w   wi

wa   with

Will went to Wellington.

sw   swept   twins

tw   swim   twist

The twins swept the path.

Essential Spellings

Work across ⟶

Read	Trace, naming letters	Write
1. we	we	
2. their	their	
3. live	live	
4. came	came	
5. have	have	
6. give	give	
7. look	look	
8. were	were	
9. about	about	
10. like	like	

1.

2. Choose 5 words from the list above and use them in 5 good sentences.

3. Now listen to your sentences and write them in your exercise book. Remember to begin with a capital letter and end with a period or question mark.

Instant words

Read the words on the vans.
Then read the sentences and link them to the vans.

(van with "my")	This van has crashed into a truck and has made a big dent.	*(van with "much")*
Much of the big van is black.	*(van with "more")*	Look at the fastest van as it passes all the rest.
(van with "make")	My dog is sitting in this van.	*(van with "made")*
The open van has more than ten men in the back.	*(van with "look")*	The man in the small van can make a lot of cash selling milk.

There and Their
Their - a possessive pronoun

1. Examples: **There** is no one **there.**
He ran here and **there.**
but
They have lost **their** cat.
Their dog is fat.

Complete the sentences by writing **there** or **their**.

1. Have you been _____?

2. _____ they are, skipping across the sands.

3. I left my bag down _____.

4. They went to _____ math lesson.

5. _____ plan is to get _____ and back before ten.

6. _____ hats are black, but _____ socks are red.

7. They all inspect _____ kit.

8. _____ is a flock of ducks at the pond.

9. _____ mom has a bad back.

10. The mom and dad make _____ kids go to bed before ten o'clock.

2. Your teacher will give you a spelling test. (See page 14.) Listen for every sound and write the words in your exercise book.

Letter J j — a consonant

ABCDEFGHIJKLMNOPQRSTUVWXYZ

Cross out the letters in alphabetical order.

jug j

1. Make the alphabet arc.
2. Auditory Introduction. (See page 12.)
3. Visual Introduction. (See page 12.)
4. Introduce the clueword and Reading/Spelling Card.
5. Use the mirror and watch the mouth say **j**. Air trapped behind the tongue is released slowly with voicing.
6. Find the letter **J** in the alphabet arc. Feel its shape.
7. Write the letter on the board and talk about how the letter is formed. Have the student trace the letter at least three times.
8. Trace and copy in green, because **j** is a consonant.

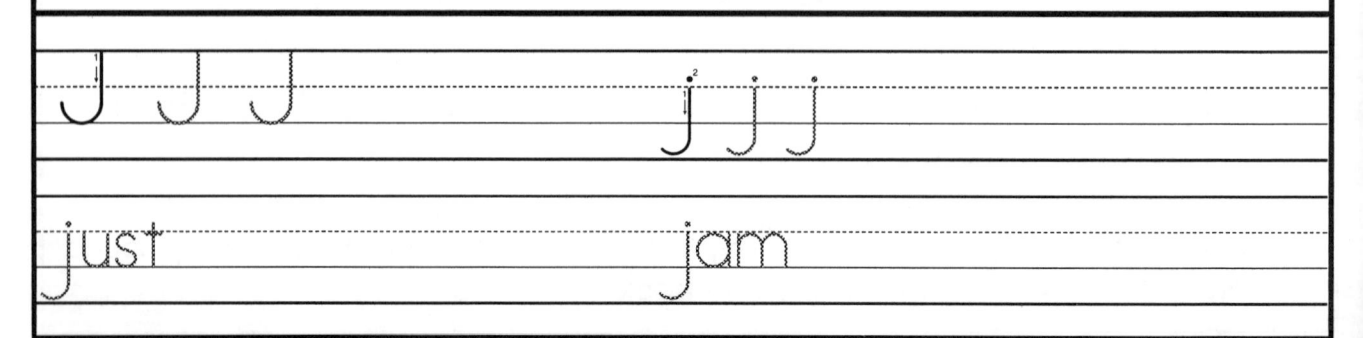

J J J   j j j

just   jam

More about letter J j

1. Listen to the teacher. (See page 14.) Write **j** in the box if you hear **j** in the word.

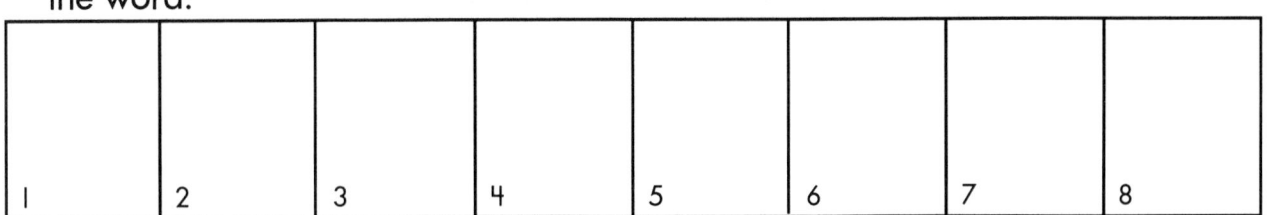

1	2	3	4	5	6	7	8

2. Write **j** on the line and read the word.

   1. ___ob   2. ___am   3. ___ump

   4. ___ust   5. ___acket 6. ___umping

   7. ___et   8. sub___ect 9. re___ect

   10. ad___ust 11. de___ected 12. un___ust

3. Your teacher will give you some of the above words. Write the words in your exercise book or finger spell them in the sandtray.

4. Circle the words with a letter **j** and read the sentences.

   1. Jim has a red jacket and a trumpet.

   2. Jill and Ross had to jump from the embankment.

   3. Jan had to adjust to the job as a consultant.

   4. Jon Smith was the dentist that wished to establish himself in Wisconsin.

   5. Jim and Jan were discontent with the subject.

More about letter J j

1. Read and solve the riddle. What am I?

   1st 2nd 3rd 4th 5th 6th 7th 8th 9th 10th 11th

   __ __ __ __ __ __ __ __ __ __ __

   My 1st is in jam and also in Jill.

   My 2nd in ant that runs to its hill.

   My 3rd is in cat, not bat, hat, or mat.

   My 4th is in kitten that traps a small rat.

   My 5th is in rabbit and rocket and run.

   My 6th is the vowel in bun, fun, and gun.

   My 7th the end when it is more than one.

   My 8th begins Simon and silent and sun.

   My 9th is in send and in mend but not sand.

   My 10th and 11th is in leg, lamb, and land.

   Can you spot me? I'll come for a jog.

   I'll yap and I'll lick you—I am a small _____.
   (Rhymes with jog!)

2. Practice your reading and spelling cards. [R|S]
3. Dictation. The teacher will read the words from Section 1. Write them in your exercise book.
4. Find and trace **j** on your caterpillar record page.

Alphabetical order
To help you use the dictionary

1. Fill in the letters that come before and after these in the alphabet.

    ___ c ___   ___ h ___   ___ q ___   ___ l ___

    ___ t ___   ___ g ___   ___ m ___   ___ j ___

    ___ s ___   ___ e ___   ___ o ___   ___ n ___

2. Here are some letters. Circle those which come **before** m.

    1.   x   l   b   w   c   a

    2.   i   p   d   n   e   t

3. Which of these come **after** m? Circle them.

    1.   n   s   t   j   d   u

    2.   b   f   q   g   x   y

4. Put these letters in alphabetical order.

    j   b   f   h   a   k   d   c   e   g   i

    ___ ___ ___ ___ ___ ___ ___ ___ ___ ___ ___

5. Put these words in alphabetical order according to the 2nd letter.

    s**p**in   S**c**otland   s**n**ip   s**t**amp   s**w**ing   s**o**ck

    ___ ___ ___ ___ ___ ___

© LDA 71 LL80103 *Reading Success Book 3*

Letter Yy — a consonant

ABCDEFGHIJKLMNOPQRSTUVWXYZ

Color the yarn yellow.

yarn y

1. Make the alphabet arc.
2. Auditory Introduction. (See page 12.)
3. Visual Introduction. (See page 12.)
4. Introduce the clueword and Reading/Spelling Card.
5. Use the mirror and watch the mouth say y. The tongue moves away from the roof of the mouth.
6. Find the letter **Y** in the alphabet arc. Feel its shape.
7. Write the letter on the board and talk about how the letter is formed. Have the student trace the letter at least three times.

8. Trace and copy in green, because **y** is a consonant.

Y Y Y   y y y

yak   yes

© LDA   72   LL80103 *Reading Success Book 3*

More about letter Y y

1. Listen to the teacher. (See page 14.) Write **y** in the box if you hear **y** in the word.

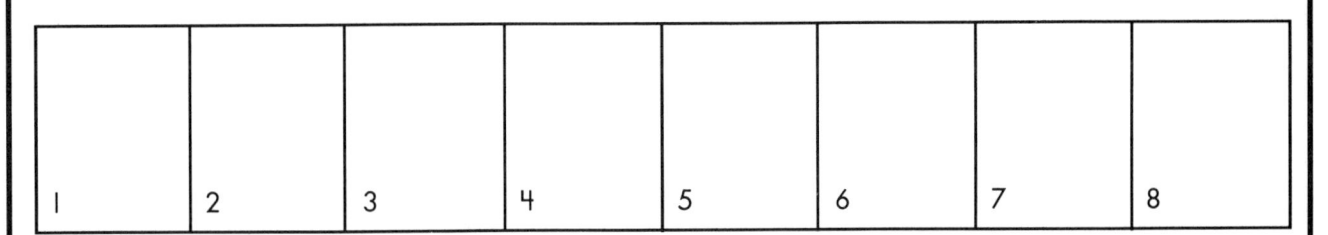

1	2	3	4	5	6	7	8

2. Write the letter **y** on the line if the picture has a **y** sound.

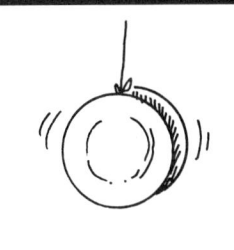

_____   _____   _____   _____

3. Fill in **y** and then read the words.

____et   ____en   ____ap   ____ank   ____ak

____ell   ____es   ____ou   ____elp   ____am

can____on   be____ond

4. Arrange the above words in alphabetical order. You will have to look at the second and third letters in some of the words.

1. _____   2. _____   3. _____

4. _____   5. _____   6. _____

7. _____   8. _____   9. _____

10. _____   11. _____   12. _____

5. Practice your reading and spelling cards.
6. Dictation. The teacher will read the words from Section 3. Write them in your exercise book.
7. Find and trace **y** on your caterpillar record page.

Question words

A question is a sentence that expects an answer. Example: Where are you?

1. Read with your teacher.

What?	When?	Why?
Where?	Which?	Who?	How?

2. How many question words can you find?

W	H	O	W	B	W	B	Y	T	S	E	L
K	T	W	H	E	R	E	O	R	T	H	M
W	R	I	E	N	X	F	D	W	H	E	N
C	G	W	H	Y	H	J	P	U	Q	I	Z
Y	X	V	W	H	W	H	W	H	I	C	H
W	H	A	T	J	D	O	R	K	P	E	C

3. Trace over the question word. Then write a question. Remember to write a **?** at the end.

What

When

Where

Who

Which

Why

How

More about long vowels

1. In open syllables vowels always have the long sound.
   Read:

   ā/pron   ē/go   ō/pen   ū/nit

   bā/sĭn   Vē/nŭs   dī/vĭng   lō/căl   mū/sĭc

2. Your teacher will give you some words. (See page 14.) Put the words you hear in the correct column. Sort them according to the vowel sound in the first syllable.

   short (Example: gŏb/lĭn)   long (Example: bī/sŏn)

3. Now take out your new pink vowel cards. Notice that the long vowel sounds have been added to the Reading Pack.
   These will now read:

   apple **a**   acorn **A**   egg **e**   equals **E**

   igloo **i**   iron **I**   octopus **o**   open **O**

   umbrella **U**   uniform **U**

More about long vowels

1. Find the open syllables. Pattern and divide these words into syllables, marking vowels long ¯ or short ˘. Example: dē/mŏn

   hijack   polo   diving   moment   judo

   vacant   viking   Roman   human   even

   stupid   Jason   emu   raven   unit

   student   propel   protect   predict   slogan

   music   siren   final   broken   omen

   relax   spiral

2. Copy these headings in your exercise book.

   A   **E**   **I**   **O**   **U**

   Now write the words in Section 1 under the correct heading according to the long vowel sound in the first syllable.

3. Add one word of your own to each column.
   Use a book or newspaper to help you. (Remember to choose words with a long vowel in the first syllable. Example: v / c v words.)

Consonant Digraph SH sh

SH   **sh**

sheep s h

1. Auditory Introduction. (See page 12.)
2. Visual Introduction. (See page 12.)
3. Introduce the clueword and Reading/Spelling Card.
4. Use the mirror and watch the mouth say sh. Air is forced between the tongue and the roof of the mouth.
5. Write the letters on the board and talk about how the letters are formed. Have the student trace the letters at least three times.

6. Trace and copy in green, because **sh** is a consonant digraph.

SH SH   sh sh

shelf   rush

7. Listen to the teacher. (See page 14.)
   White **sh** in the box if you hear sh in the word.

1	2	3	4	5	6	7	8

More about consonant digraph SH sh

1. Read the **sh** words to your teacher.

she	wish	fish	ship	dash	mesh
shrub	shrimp	smash	clash	gash	shed
trash	flesh	rash	shot	shut	fresh

2. Write **sh** under the pictures which begin with **sh**.

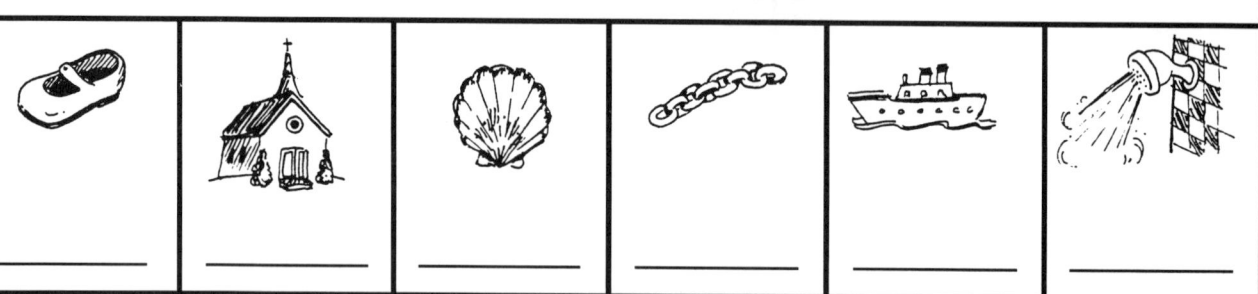

3. Write **sh** under the pictures which end with **sh**.

4. Circle the **sh** words and read these sentences to your teacher. You should find 21 words.

   1. He kicks him in the shins in the rush to get the ball.
   2. The ship will crash on the rocks and sink.
   3. He can smash the glass and grab the bag with the cash in it.
   4. He got shellshock from the flash and the blast.
   5. When she is on the ship, she will fish for fresh shrimp.
   6. Sam ran into the shrub and has a gash on his shin.
   7. Pam has a rash where she had the shot.

More about consonant digraph SH sh

1. Pattern, divide, code the vowels, and read these words to your teacher.

| shamrock | publish | Yiddish | Oshkosh |
| shipping | blandish | snapshot | establish |

2. Read the clue. Write the word in the blank.

fish   shamrock   shop   shrink   shrimp

1. It swims and has fins _____

2. To get small in the wash _____

3. The emblem of the Irish _____

4. A man sells things in it _____

5. A shellfish _____

3. Read these sentences. Your teacher will give these sentences for dictation. Write them in your exercise book.

1. The fish shop is shut.
   I wish it was open.

2. She got a snapshot of the song thrush.

3. The best dish is on the shelf.

4. She spends her cash on trash.

Crisis for the Pilot

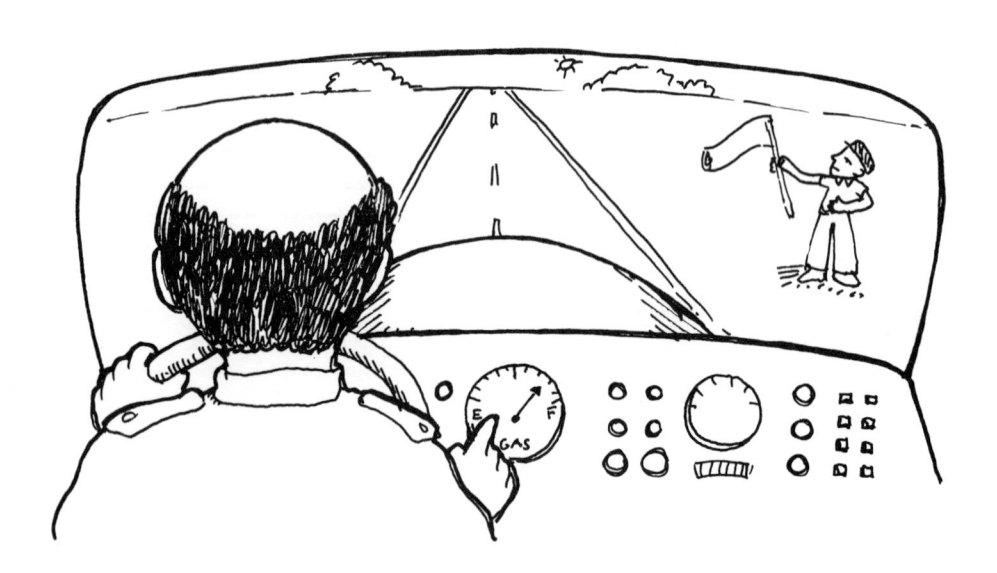

1

"We need gas," thinks Simon, the pilot. As Simon begins to land his craft he sees that he does not need gas.

2

At that moment he decides not to stop. Simon pulls back the stick and lifts the craft up into the mist. The silent flick of a button sends back a signal to traffic control and says, "We are on our way to Poland."

1. Underline the v / c v words. You should find 9.

2. What was the pilot called? _____

3. What is a crisis? _____
   _____

4. In which continent is Poland found? _____

5. How is the signal sent back to traffic control?
   _____

6. What happens in the end? Finish the story in your exercise book or tell it on tape.

Handwriting Practice
Trace and copy.

j   job   just

ja   Jack and Jill jump.

y   yap   yell

ye   Yaks do not yap.

sh   shell

she   shelf

She wishes at the wishing well.

She wants to do the washing.

Flag design

Listen to the teacher and follow instructions. (See page 14.)
Make sure you have a pencil, ruler, and colored pencils.

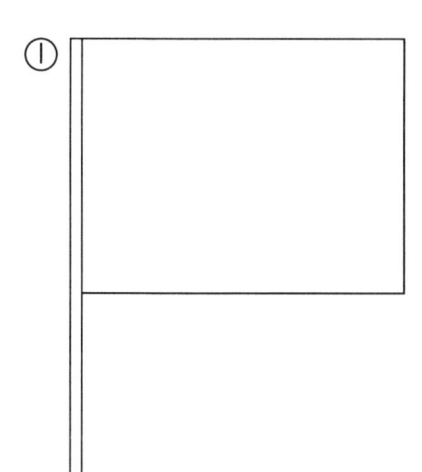

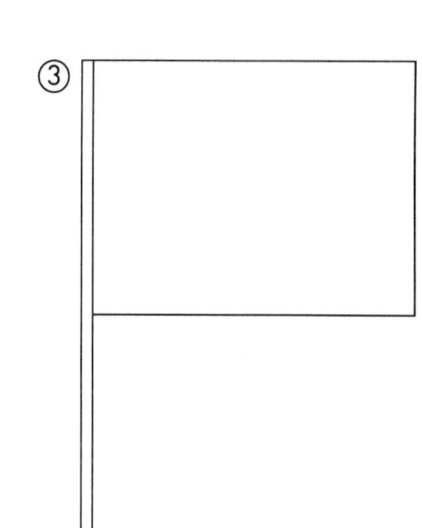

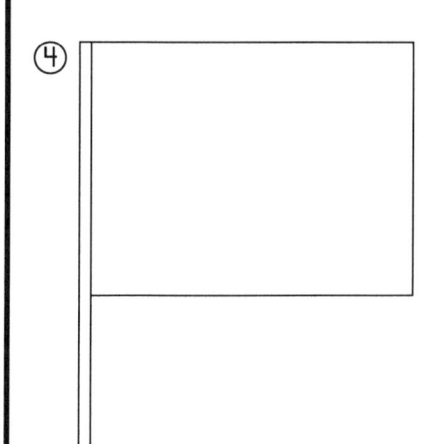

① ② ③

④ ⑤ ⑥

Nouns

A noun is a name of a person, place, or thing.

1. Read these **nouns** (names) and then write them in the correct column.

   Notice that a person's name and the names of towns and countries always begin with a capital letter. They are **proper nouns**.

   STUBBY

2. NOUNS

goblin	student	Scotland
Dublin	Batman	goddess
Madrid	windmill	Holland
dustbin	milkman	sandpit
Sweden	magnet	basket

3.

Person	Place	Thing
Examples: student	Holland	basket

Letter "a" saying o
The letter **a** after **w** usually makes an **o** sound

ABCDEFGHIJKLMNOPQRSTUVWXYZ

wasp   **w o**

1. Put the **w** in front of the **a** on the wasp's wing.

2. Read with your teacher.

   1. want   2. wasp   3. Walton
   4. wand   5. swap   6. swat
   7. swan   8. wallet 9. wash

3. Underline the letters in Section 2 which make the **w o** sound.

4. Now solve the crossword. Use words from Section 2 above.

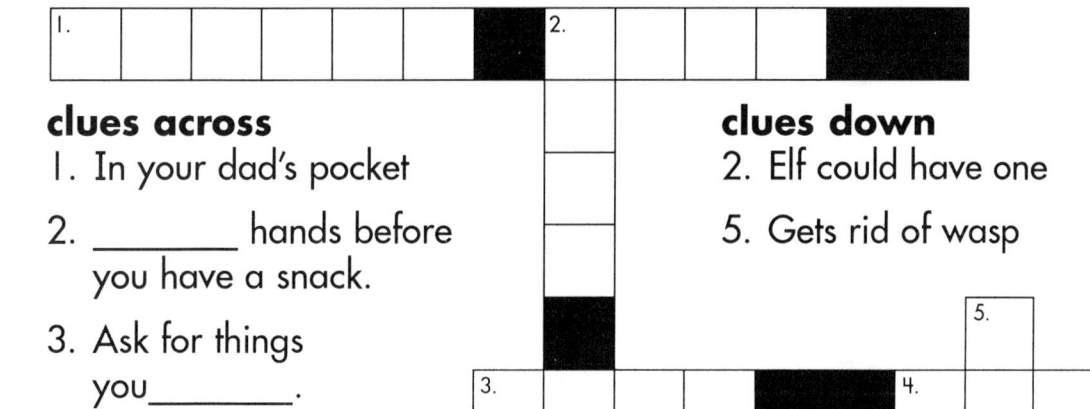

clues across
1. In your dad's pocket
2. _____ hands before you have a snack.
3. Ask for things you _____.
4. Swims (has long neck)

clues down
2. Elf could have one
5. Gets rid of wasp

85   Reading Success Book 3

Winston and Wilfred Go to the Windmill

1

The twins Winston and Wilfred went up the hill to see the windmill. It was a long trek from the bottom to the top, and the windmill was so small and distant.

2

Up and up they went, until they were panting and getting hot.

"Let's stop now and have a drink," said Winston. Wilfred had a can of soda in his rucksack.

They drank it all and then plodded on up to the summit.

At the top of the hill, the windmill was fantastic. The strong wind was from the west and the vast wings of the windmill were spinning fast, humming and strumming in the strong gusts.

"How can it be so big? Let's see if we can get in," said Winston.

"I can't open it," said Wilfred as he lifted the padlock.

"We must not be vandals," said Winston.

The sun was beginning to sink in the west. All of a sudden, a silent bat swept past in the dusk, skimming the top of Winston's cap and making him duck. "Let's get back before sunset so that we can still see the path," Winston said. They trotted down as fast as they could, tripping and stumbling on the rocks as they went.

Comprehension Questions

Write your answers in your exercise book.

1. Why did they run down the hill so fast? Discuss this with a friend.

2. Was the windmill small?

3. What is a summit? Use your dictionary to find out.

4. How many words can you think of which rhyme with "drank"?

5. What is a bat? (Not the one you use to hit a ball.)

6. Have you ever had a frightening experience? Write or tell about it.

Sound Pictures ⟶ Words

1. Use Spelling Pack Cards to make these Sound Pictures.	2. Turn the cards over. Tell your hand what to write, naming the letters.	3. Write the word.
Look Say	Listen Name the letters (Tell your hand what to write.)	Write
1. w o n t	-w-a-n-t-	1. want
2. w o z		2.
3. b A s i n		3.
4. v E n u s		4.
5. j a k e t		5.
6. t A k e n		6.
7. sh e l		7.

Essential Spellings

Work across ⟶

Read	Trace, naming letters	Write
1. make	make	
2. made	made	
3. they	they	
4. she	she	
5. you	you	
6. more	more	
7. because	because	
8. what	what	
9. any	any	
10. many	many	

Word families and rhyming

1. Circle the words which rhyme in each group below.

Example:

(ring)	dish	duck	broth	tank	belt
(sing)	fish	stick	froth	pink	felt
hang	flash	luck	moth	bank	help
(thing)	wish	pluck	bath	sank	melt

sang	cash	bunk	math	sink	at
tang	smash	sunk	path	wink	rat
bang	wish	frank	both	pink	back
fang	mesh	sink	bath	plank	scat

2. Fill in the vowel to complete these rhyming pairs.

| much | lock | bell | bath | silt |
| s__ch | s__ck | sp__ll | p__th | w__lt |

Word families and rhyming

1. Read these groups of words. Circle the one that is different from the other three. Then write the family pattern.

Example:				
black	(lick)	crack	stack	ack
beg	leg	wag	peg	
moth	pith	froth	broth	
ash	rash	clash	rush	
mess	dress	cross	less	
drum	grim	plum	sum	
yell	bell	smell	hull	
shrink	yank	ink	wink	
jump	hump	thump	limp	
bang	rung	hung	flung	

Letter Q q — a consonant

1. Join the dots in alphabetical order. What have you got?

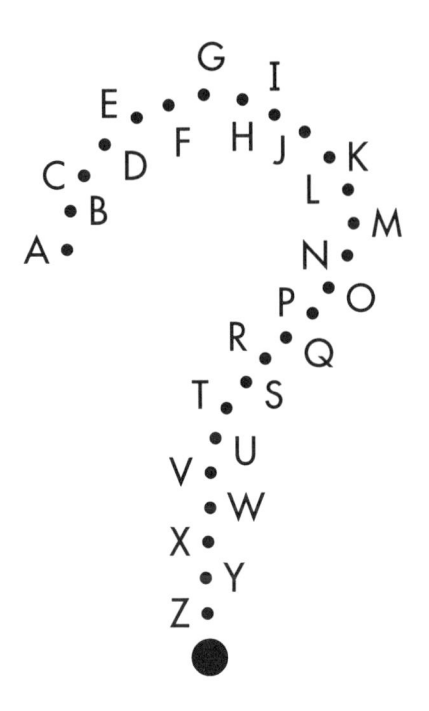

question

kw

Question is the clueword because it begins with **kw**.

2. Auditory Introduction. (See page 12.)
3. Visual Introduction. (When you see the letter "q" you will always see the letter "u" right after it. The letter "u" is not considered a vowel when it follows the letter "q". See page 12.)
4. The **qu** has two sounds. Say **k** + **w** = **kw**.
5. Write the letter on the board and talk about how the letters are formed. Have the student trace the letters at least three times.

6. Trace and copy in green, because **qu** serves as a consonant.

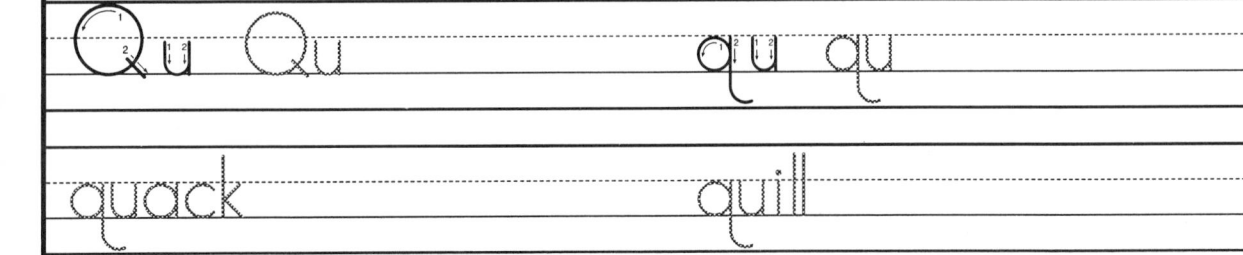

Qu Qu   qu qu

quack   quill

© LDA   LL80103 *Reading Success Book 3*

More combination QU qu

1. Listen to the teacher. (See page 15.) Write **qu** in the box if you hear a **kw** sound in the word.

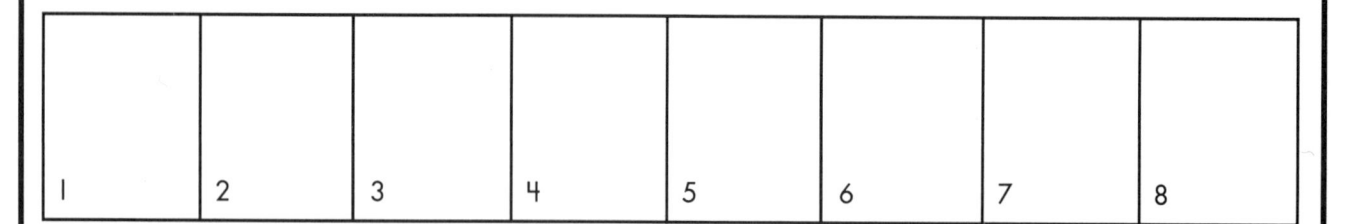

1	2	3	4	5	6	7	8

2. Read these words to your teacher.

quick   quits   quint   quell   quill   quilt

quack   squid   request   squint   equips   Quentin

3. Circle the **qu** words and read.

   1. Quentin squints.

   2. Tom is quick at squash.

   3. Tim's equipment cost a hundred quid.

   4. The ducks quack.

   5. Jan has a quilt on her bed.

   6. Quinn is on a quest for the best squid.

4. Your teacher will give you some of the above sentences for dictation. Write the sentences in your exercise book.

5. Write these words in your exercise book in alphabetical order.

   quit   quack   quell   squid   request

   squint   equips   Quentin   quill   squash

6. The teacher will read words from Section 5 for dictation.

More about QU qu

1. Write a **qu** under the picture if you hear a **kw** sound.

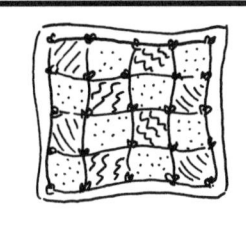

2. Fill in the missing letters with **qu** and read the words.

    ____ick   ____its   ____int   ____ell

    ____ill   ____ilt   ____ack   s____id

    re____est   s____int   e____ips   ____entin

3. Make the words by combining the letters.

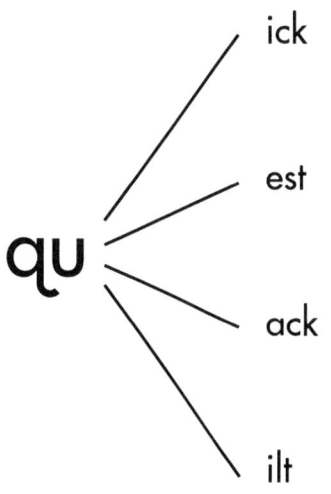

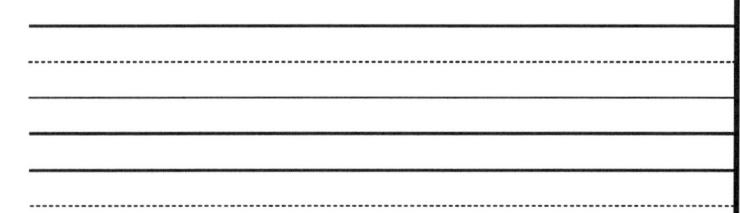

    qu — ick
       — est
       — ack
       — ilt

4. Put each of the words from Section 2 in a sentence of your own. Write them in your exercise book. Remember to use capital letters and periods or question marks.

5. Find and trace **q** on your caterpillar record page.

The doubling rule

1. Write the vc pattern; split; read

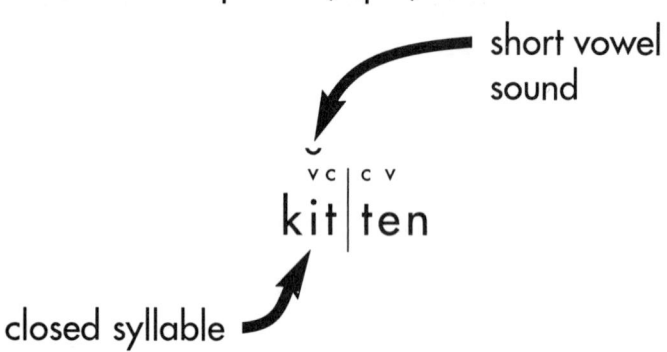

    kĭt|ten — short vowel sound, closed syllable

    mū|sic — long vowel sound, open syllable

    Rule: When adding endings, always check the vccv pattern if you need to keep the vowel short.

    Examples: Skip + ing = skĭp|ping ✓ correct

    Skip + ing = skī|ping ✗ wrong

2. Now do these words sums.

    stop + ing = _____

    rest + ed = _____

    hand + ed = _____

    shop + ing = _____

    quit + ing = _____

    think + ing = _____

3. **Rule:** Spell; vc pattern and split; read; check.

    Example: v̆ c / c v   v̄ / c v

Suffixes and the doubling rule

Remember to check the vc/cv pattern.

1. Add the endings (suffixes) to complete the words.

Examples: skip + ing = skip|ping ✓ correct

rest + ed = res|ted ✓ correct

mad + ness = madd|ness ✗ wrong

2. Now try these:

clap + ing = _____

fill + ing = _____

mad + est = _____

hunt + ed = _____

ship + ment = _____

sad + ness = _____

sit + ing = _____

hand + ed = _____

big + est = _____

fit + ness = _____

wit + less = _____

Letter X x — a consonant

ABCDEFGHIJKLMNOPQRSTUVWXYZ

box **k s**

Box ends with **k s**

1. Make the alphabet arc.
2. Auditory Introduction. (See page 12.)
3. Visual Introduction. (See page 12.)
4. Introduce the clueword and Reading/Spelling Card.
5. Use the mirror and watch the mouth say **k s**. Note that **x** is one letter but it makes two sounds **k** **s**.
6. **X** is mostly used at the end of words or syllables.
7. Find the letter **X** in the alphabet arc. Feel its shape.
8. Write the letter on the board and talk about how the letter is formed. Have the student trace the letter at least three times.

9. Trace and copy in green, because **x** is a consonant.

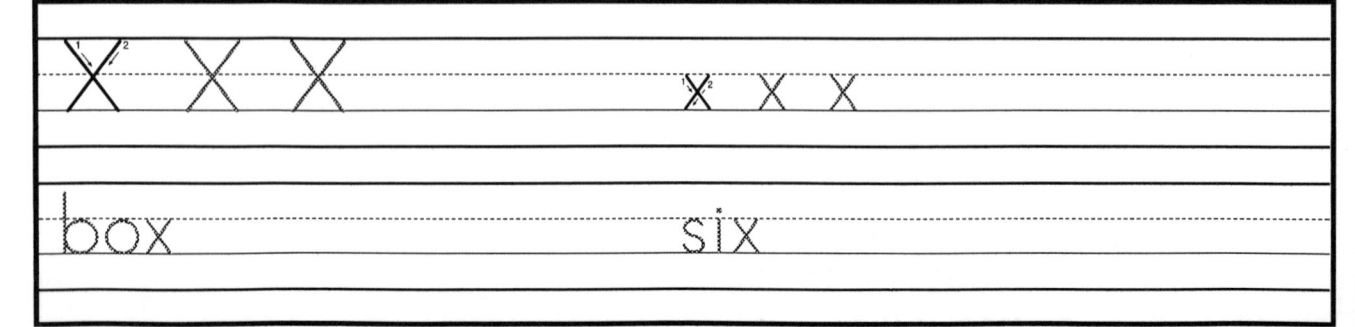

X X X   X X X

box   six

© LDA   98   LL80103 *Reading Success Book 3*

More about letter X x

1. Listen to the teacher. (See page 15.) Write **x** in the box if you hear **k s** in the word.

1	2	3	4	5	6	7	8

2. Read these words to your teacher.

box	mix	fox	fix	ax	tax
next	wax	context	six	extra	sexton
Rex	sax	fax	index	expert	appendix
expel	affix	convex	expand	text	sixth

3. Read and write the number of syllables you hear in each word.

Examples: fix (1)   fixes (2)

1. index ( )   2. next ( )   3. mixes ( )
4. box ( )   5. Rex ( )   6. jinx ( )
7. fox ( )   8. expect ( )   9. waxwing ( )

4. Circle each word that has an **x** and read the sentences to your teacher.

1. Rex did not expect to see the fox.
2. The doctor had to fix his appendix.
3. The box was filled with mixes.
4. The text had no index.

5. Dictation. Your teacher will give you the sentences in Section 4 for dictation. Write the sentences in your exercise book.

More about letter X x

1. Write the word on the line for each picture.

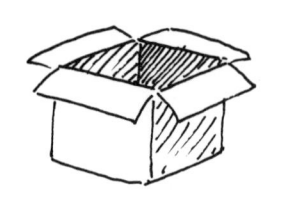

_____	_____	_____	_____

2. Write the words on page 99, Section 2 in alphabetical order.

a b c d e f g h i j k l m n o p q r s t u v w x y z

1. _____ 2. _____

3. _____ 4. _____

5. _____ 6. _____

7. _____ 8. _____

9. _____ 10. _____

11. _____ 12. _____

3. Note that plural words (more than one) always end in **es** after **x**.

six   sixes   tax   taxes   fox   foxes

Write the plural of:

fax_____   box_____

4. Read and fill in the answer. Choose words from Section 2. You may need to add –es.

1. You pack things in them. _____

2. They attack chickens. _____

3. I went into the hospital to have it fixed. _____

The past tense of the verb
Suffix –ed

Adding suffix –ed to the end of a verb shows an action has happened in the past.

Examples: He **kicked** the ball.   **kick + ed**

   I **asked** him to come.   **ask + ed**

1. Read these words and listen carefully to the last sound.

   mended [e][d]   yelled [d]   kicked [t]

   If you try to spell the word as it sounds you will get it wrong.

   Examples: mendid ✗   yelld ✗   kickt ✗

   So when you hear one of these sounds at the end of a verb, remember to write –ed.

   Write each word from the Sound Pictures.

2.
   1. j u m p t   jumped
   2. f i l d
   3. l i f t e d
   4. st o p t
   5. h a ng d
   6. l o k t
   7. f u n d e d
   8. a s k t

More about suffix -ed

1. Add –ed to the verb and use this past tense form to complete each sentence.

   1. fill **d**

      Mom _____ the milk jug.

   2. sprint **e** **d**

      He _____ down the track as fast as he could go.

   3. jump **t**   dress **t**

      Jack _____ up and got _____ when the bell rang.

   4. gang **d**

      The thugs _____ up on Jim and Mick.

2. Read the sentences and look at the base word and suffix that come together to make the word. When you have a vowel suffix and a base word that ends in two consonants you **just add the suffix.**

He **kicked** the ball.	kick + ed
I **asked** him to come.	ask + ed
The bug got **stomped**.	stomp + ed
He **missed** his mom.	miss + ed
Tom **yelled** back at Rick.	yell + ed
They **rested** in the soft grass.	rest + ed

More about suffix –ed

1. Remember if you are adding a vowel suffix to a base word that ends in a short vowel and one consonant, you must double the final consonant.

   1. ship + ed = _____

   2. rob + ed = _____

   3. trim + ed = _____

   4. star + ed = _____

   5. grip + ed = _____

   6. snap + ed = _____

   7. slim + ed = _____

   8. scrub + ed = _____

   9. kick + ed = _____

   10. ask + ed = _____

   11. miss + ed = _____

   12. rest + ed = _____

2. Practice your reading and spelling pack cards.

Sound Pictures → Words

1. Use spelling pack cards to make these sound pictures.	2. Turn the cards over. Tell your hand what to write, naming the letters.	3. Write the word.
Look Say	Listen Name the letters (Tell your hand what to write)	Write
1. kwik	-q-u-i-c-k-	1. quick
2. kwak		2.
3. kwest		3.
4. skwid		4.
5. yeld		5.
6. taks		6.
7. skwint		7.
8. skwosht		8.

Punctuation

1. First read this story. Then read it again, putting a period in the places marked by a square.

Now read it aloud with your teacher. Notice how the periods tell you when to pause. Without the periods it does not make sense. That is because a period signals the end of a sentence. A sentence is a string of words which makes sense. Periods divide the story into sentences which you can understand.

Help!
A Bad Dog

The kids (ran) across the grass as fast as they could go ☐ Tim fell in the mud ☐ He picked himself up and ran on ☐ Jason was puffing and grunting a bit ☐ He still kept up with them all ☐

They had almost gotten to the wall ☐ The strong bulldog was galloping along after them ☐

Yasmin was quick and got to the wall before the rest of the gang ☐ She began scrambling up to the top ☐ Then Jan got there ☐ Yasmin helped to pull her up ☐

At last all of them but Jason were on top of the wall ☐ Then he saw the black dog ☐ He yelled and kicked ☐ Tim dragged Jason onto the top of the wall to sit with the rest of them ☐ The dog could not get at them ☐

They had to sit there until the dog sat down ☐
Then they slid down or jumped from the wall ☐ It
was not a bad dog ☐ It was a kind dog ☐

The End

2. Do you remember that every sentence must have a verb? Go back to the beginning and put a red circle around every verb (doing or action word) that you can find. The first one has been done for you. Next, put a green circle around every noun (naming word).

Letter Z z — a consonant

A B C D E F G H I J K L M N O P Q R S T U V W X Y Z

zebra **Z**

1 2 3 4
      • 5
      • 6
     • 7
    • 8
 •   •   •   •
 9 10 11 12

1. Make the alphabet arc.
2. Auditory Introduction. (See page 12.)
3. Visual Introduction. (See page 12.)
4. Introduce the clueword and Reading/Spelling Cards.
5. Use the mirror and watch the mouth say **z**. This is a voiced sound.
6. Find the letter **z** in the alphabet arc. Feel its shape.
7. Write the letter on the board and talk about how the letter is formed. Have the student trace the letter at least three times.

8. Trace and copy in green, because **z** is a consonant.

Z Z Z   z z z

Zigzag   zebra

© LDA   109   LL80103 Reading Success Book 3

More about letter Z z

1. Listen to the teacher. (See page 15.) Write **z** in the box if you hear **z** in the word.

1	2	3	4	5	6	7	8

2. Read these words to your teacher.

zip   zig   zag   zap   zest   zigzag

quiz   whiz   buzz   fizz   fuzz   jazz

zenith   frozen   crazy   lazy

3. Read the story to your teacher.

    The wasp came buzzing onto Justin's muffin, just as he put it to his lips. "Hang on!" yelled Rex, swatting the wasp and the muffin onto the grass. "Thanks, Pal," said Justin. "I'm not fond of insect jam!" The wasp went zigzagging onto the dish of rock buns. "If he doesn't push off, he'll be squashed," said Justin.

More about letter Z z

1. Read.

   zip   zest   zap   zigzag

   pins   his   tins   dogs

   has   is   was   as

   Which letters make the **z** sound? 1. _____ 2. _____

2. Write the words from the Sound Pictures.

   z i p _____   **h i z** _____

   p i n z _____   **h a z** _____

   z e s t _____   **z i g z a g** _____

3. Add the suffixes to these base words. Do you need to double the final consonant?

buzz	+	er	=	_____
mud	+	y	=	_____
plump	+	est	=	_____
strip	+	ed	=	_____
shift	+	ing	=	_____

4. Practice your reading and spelling cards. [R|S]

5. The teacher will read the words from Section 1 for dictation. Write them in your exercise book.

6. Find and trace **z** on your caterpillar record page.

Capital letters
How to write them correctly

1. These are the last of the letters you have learned. Trace and copy.

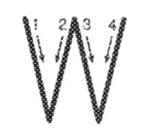

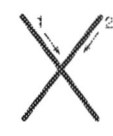

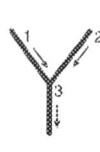

   F _____ G _____ J _____ K _____

   Q _____ U _____ V _____ W _____

   X _____ Y _____ Z _____

2. Write the capital letter next to the clueword picture.

   Example:

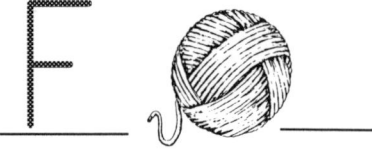

   ⠙ F _____   (yarn) _____   (windmill) _____   (teapot) _____

   ? _____   (umbrella) _____   (box) _____   (zebra) _____

   (van) _____   (jug) _____   (soap) _____

3. Your teacher will give you a spelling test. (See page 15.) Listen for every sound and write the words in your exercise book.

Adjectives

Adjectives are words which describe nouns.

1. Read these adjectives.

black	pink	red	mad	stupid	wet
small	thin	quick	plump	soft	fat
strong	silent	hot	big	stinging	jumping

2. Choose one adjective from Section 1 to describe each noun.

A _____   A _____

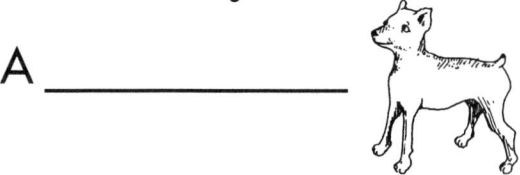

A _____ squirrel   A _____ bull

A _____   A _____

A _____ fox   A _____ yak

A _____ rabbit   A _____

A  _____   A _____ kitten

A _____ gull   A _____

A  _____   A _____ duck

A _____ shrimp   A _____

Alphabet Review

1. Write the alphabet in the boxes. Write one letter in each box, but write both capital and lowercase forms.
   Example:

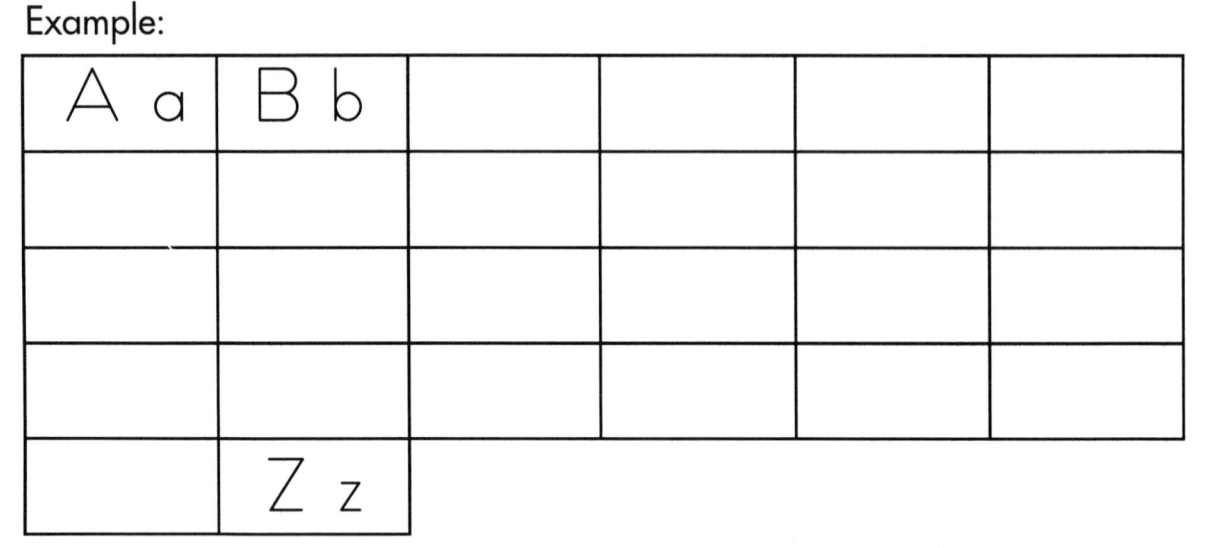

A a	B b				
	Z z				

Give your answers as both capital and lowercase letters.

2. Begin at A a. Move 3 boxes to the right.
   Which box are you on? _____

3. Begin at X x. Move 5 boxes to the left.
   Which box are you on? _____

4. Color the vowel boxes red.

5. Color pink the letter which can be a vowel or a consonant.

6. Color the first letter of your name blue.
   (If it is colored, draw around the box in blue.)

7. Which letter comes before Q q? _____

8. What is the letter after P p? _____

9. What letter is directly above N n? _____

10. Which letter is directly under G g? _____

Use a dictionary and see how quickly you can find the list of words which begin with:

T   M   E   A   Z

Handwriting Practice
Trace and copy.

q					qu

squint				Quentin wants to quit.

sc					wasp

osc				Russ has six boxes.

z					zip

ze

The wasp buzzes.

Jazz is music.

Final -ff

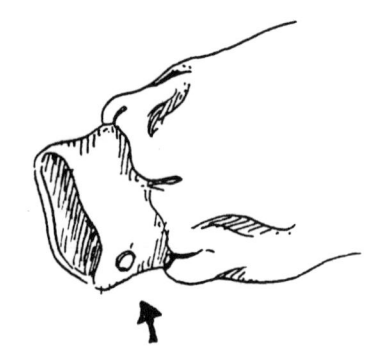

cuff

1. Auditory Introduction. (See page 12.)
2. Visual Introduction. (See page 12.)
3. Introduce the clueword and Reading/Spelling Card.
4. Concept: At the end of a one-syllable word, after a short vowel, use **ff** when you hear the word end in **f**.
5. Write the letters on the board and talk about how the letters are formed.

6. Trace and copy in green, because **ff** serves as a consonant.

7. Listen to the teacher. (See page 15.)
   Write **ff** in the box if you hear **f** at the end of the word.

1	2	3	4	5	6	7	8

More about ll, ss, ff, ck

1. **Rule:** At the end of a one-syllable word, after a short vowel, use **ff** when you hear the *f* sound. Code the vowels and read these words to your teacher.

cuff	sniff	doff	gaff
puff	cliff	toff	staff
snuff	quiff	scoff	quaff (**a** says *o* here.)

2. Trace the letters adding **ff** to complete the words.

   1. cli_____   2. sco_____   3. blu_____

   4. qua_____   5. do_____   6. to_____

   7. sni_____   8. sta_____

3. Code the vowels and read these words to your teacher.

běll	kiss	cliff	sick
spill	class	bluff	track
grill	glass	staff	quick
smell	floss	muff	lock
dwell	Swiss	sniff	neck
small	press	gruff	pack

4. How many beats can you hear in each word in Section 3?

   Check the box [1] [2] [3]

5. **Rule:** At the **end** of a **one-syllable** word after a **short vowel sound** use **ll, ss, ff,** or **ck**.

More about ll, ss, ff, ck

1. **Rule:** At the **end** of a **one-syllable** word after a **short vowel sound** use **ll, ss, ff,** or **ck.**

2. Add **ll, ss, ff,** or **ck** to complete the words.

   1. Ja____ and Ji____ went up the hi____ to hunt for their bla____ cat.

   2. They spotted some flu____ at the top of the cli____.

   3. "Oh no!" sobbed Ji____. "Don't sni____," said Ja____.

   4. He called, "Pu____, Pu____, Pu____, come ba____."

   5. The flu____ sprang up and trotted along the track.

   6. "He's we____," yelled Ji____.

   7. She picked up the bla____ cat and gave him a ki____.

3. Write the word for the Sound Pictures.

   kw i l _____   sk o f _____

   dr e s _____   gr a s _____

   sh a k _____   d u l _____

   k u f _____   th i k _____

Hugo the Tulip Addict

1

Hugo the hippo was cross. He was sulking. He was fond of tulips but he had not had even one pass his lips for so long.

2

If he did not have tulips before long, he would crash about and bring down the walls of his pen.

He began to stamp and butt his tank, making a big racket.

His keeper fed him on a dish of irises, but he did not go for them at all. They did not get past his tonsils. He spat a big basin of them all about his pen and then went splashing off into his pond.

This offended the staff. They hated to see Hugo so upset and were sad that Hugo had not taken to the irises.

One of the staff said, "We'll see if Hugo can gulp a cactus." This was no problem. Hugo had a big gulp, and the bucket of cactus went down.

All the staff felt so glad. "A big clap for Hugo," they said, for they all had a soft spot for him and were glad to see he was not cross at the moment.

7

The problem was going to be in getting lots of cactus plants from a hot land. Could they send for some from Uganda that would fill Hugo's big tum?

8

Stubby's cross country run

Shake and throw a die and read the notices as you go. (See page 20.)

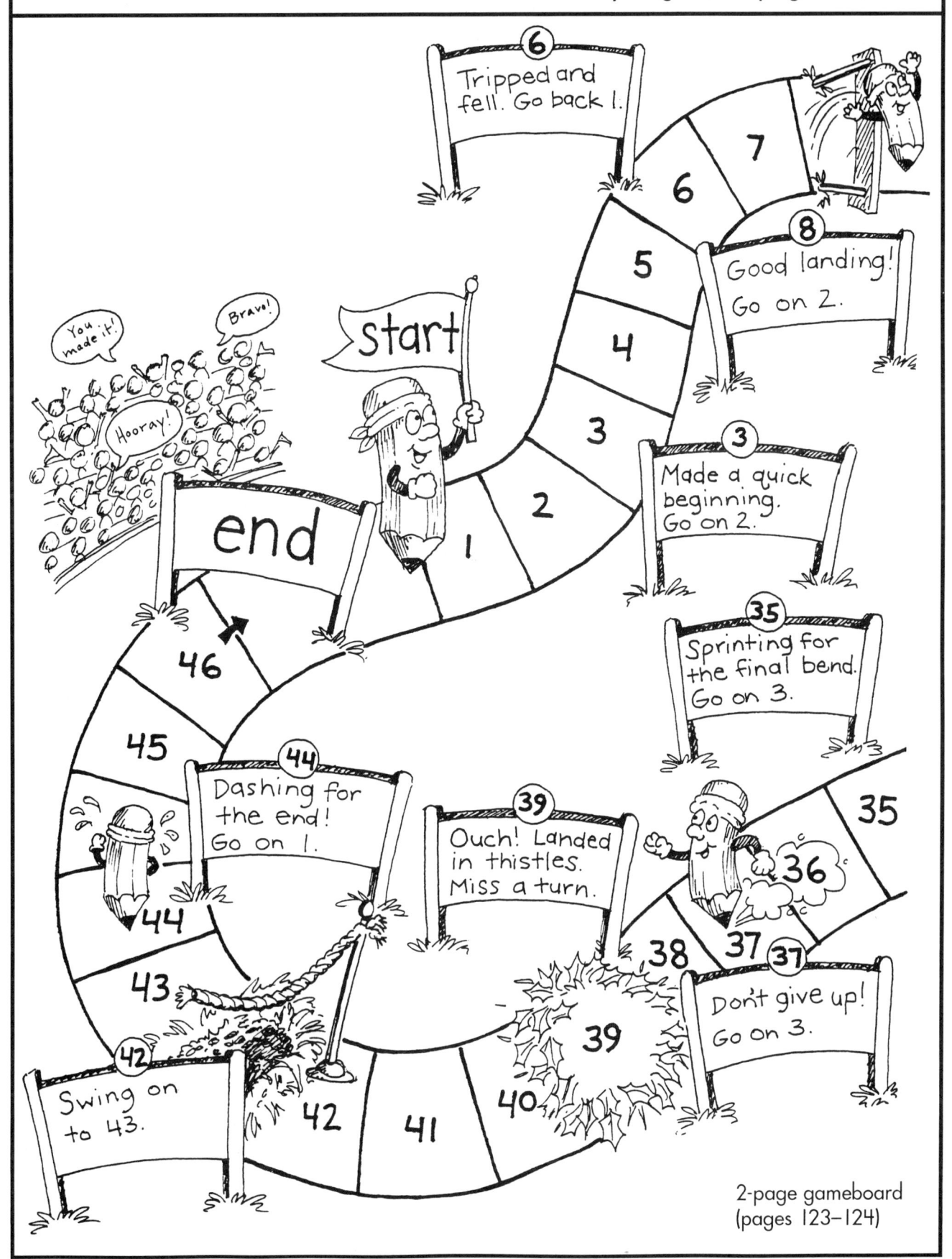

6 Tripped and fell. Go back 1.

8 Good landing! Go on 2.

3 Made a quick beginning. Go on 2.

35 Sprinting for the final bend. Go on 3.

44 Dashing for the end! Go on 1.

39 Ouch! Landed in thistles. Miss a turn.

37 Don't give up! Go on 3.

42 Swing on to 43.

You made it!
Bravo!
Hooray!

2-page gameboard
(pages 123–124)

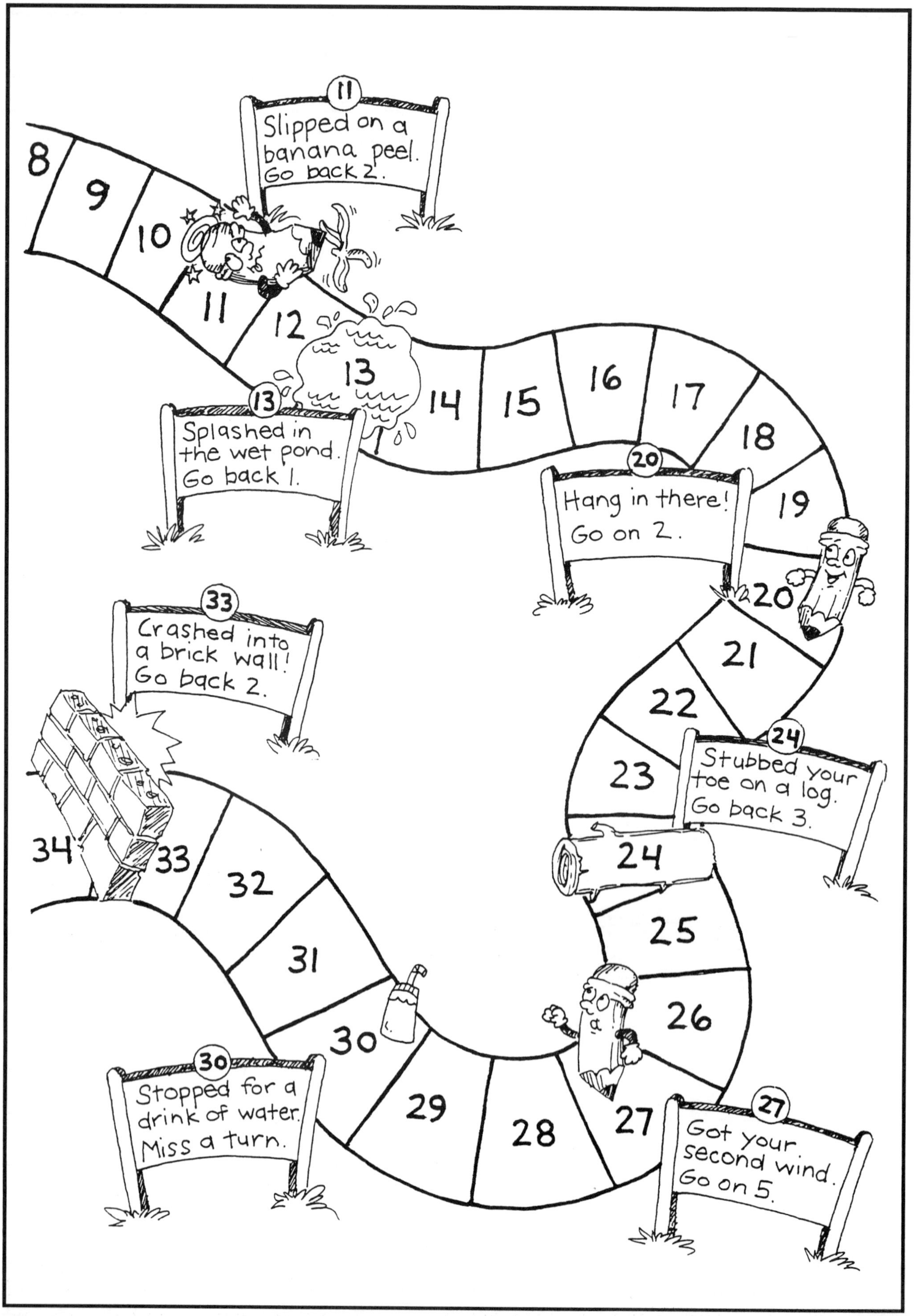
11 Slipped on a banana peel. Go back 2.
13 Splashed in the wet pond. Go back 1.
20 Hang in there! Go on 2.
24 Stubbed your toe on a log. Go back 3.
27 Got your second wind. Go on 5.
30 Stopped for a drink of water. Miss a turn.
33 Crashed into a brick wall! Go back 2.
8
9
10
11
12
13
14
15
16
17
18
19
20
21
22
23
24
25
26
27
28
29
30
31
32
33
34

Consonant digraph Ch ch

B C E G H J N P R V Y Z

cherry **c h**

Fill in the missing letters.

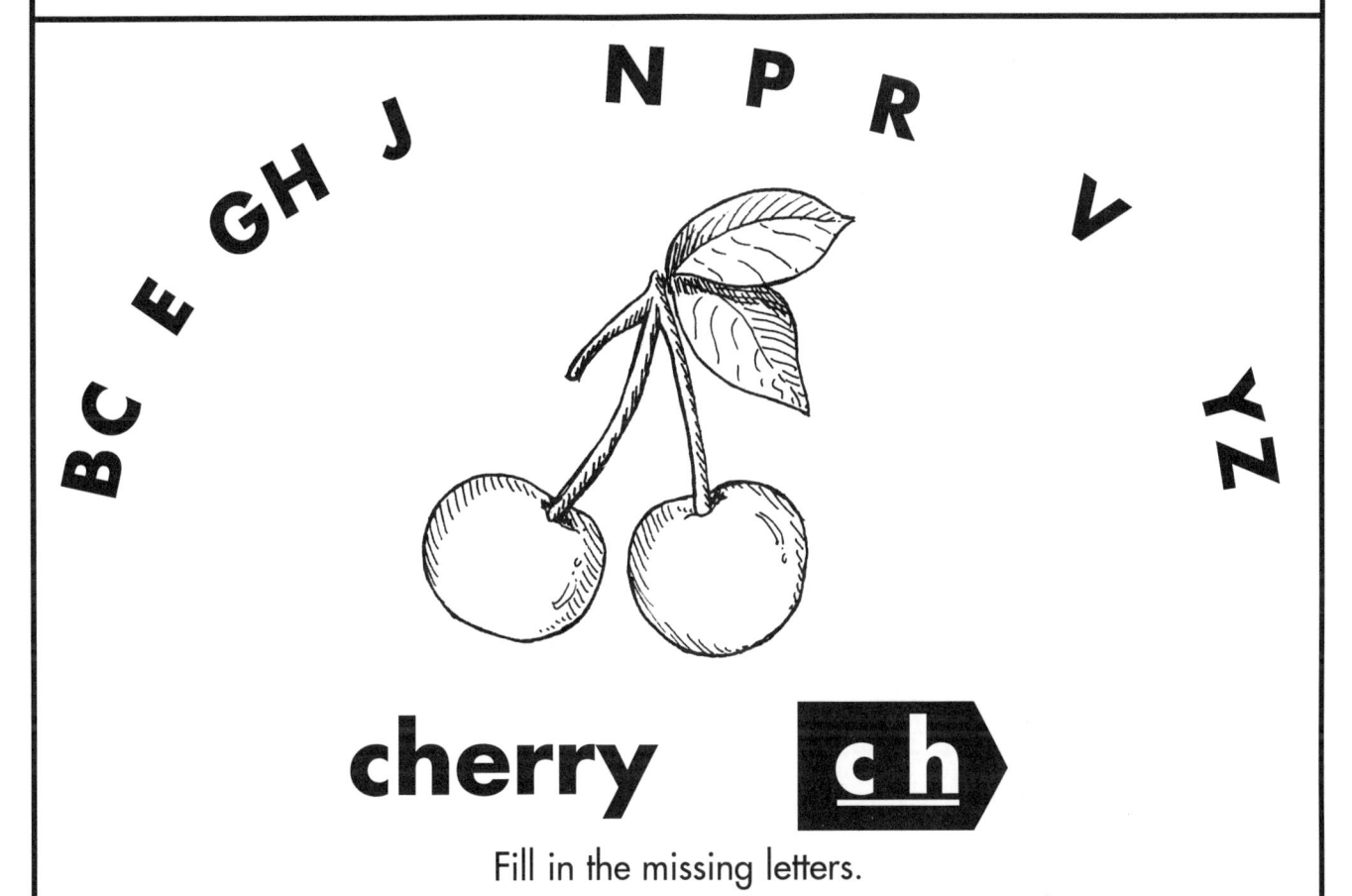

1. Make the alphabet arc.
2. Auditory Introduction. (See page 12.)
3. Visual Introduction. (See page 12.)
4. Introduce the clueword and Reading/Spelling Cards.
5. Use the mirror and watch the mouth say **ch**. Air trapped behind the tongue is released slowly.
6. Write the letters on the board and talk about how the letters are formed. Have the student trace the letters at least three times.

7. Trace and copy in green, because **ch** is a consonant digraph.

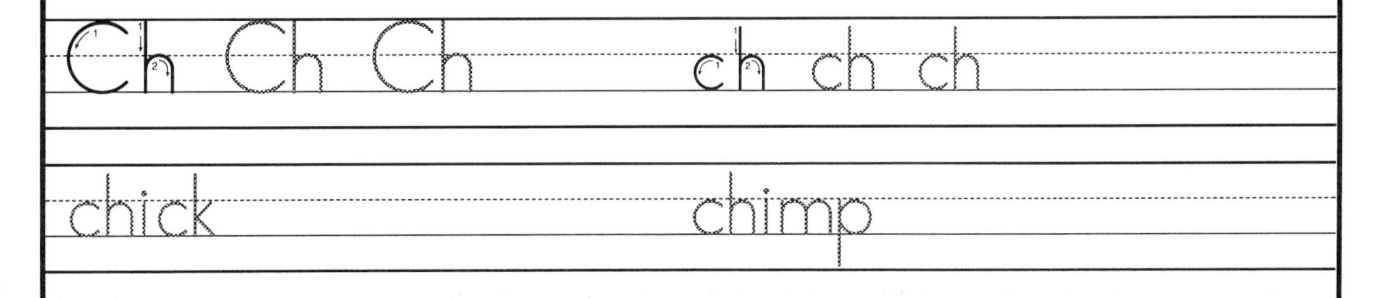

Ch Ch Ch   ch ch ch

chick   chimp

More about ch

1. Listen to the teacher. (See page 15.) Write the **ch** in the box if you hear **ch** in the word.

1	2	3	4	5	6	7	8

2. Circle the letters which say **ch**. You should find 5.

sh	ck	CH	cr	st	ch	th	j
Cl	sp	ch	SH	cl	SP	sh	CK
ch	Dr	TH	CR	gl	oh	CO	ch

3. Write **ch** under the pictures which begin with **ch**.
   Write **sh** under the pictures which begin with **sh**.

4. Fill in the **ch** and read these words to your teacher.

   ___op   ___imp   ___eck   ___icken

   bun___   ___um   ___ess   mun___

   ___amp   ___ill   ___est   ran___

5. Your teacher will give you some of these words for finger spelling in the sand tray.

6. Practice your reading and spelling cards.

Max and His Gang of Chimps

Max and the chimps were resting. They were hidden in the bushes.

It was so hot. They sucked milk from coconuts and sat still, thinking.

3

Bad chimps were sitting on a rock just across the hill. The bad chimps wanted to take the coconuts. Max must help his chimps get to the den.

4

Max was thinking about this. He would have to be quick and make a plan before the bad chimps jumped off the rock to take their coconuts.

---

1. Read the sentences to your teacher. Your teacher will give the sentences for dictation. Use your exercise book.

    1. The chimps sat and chatted.
    2. Max chomped a bunch of bananas.
    3. He chucked one to a small chimp.
    4. A hush fell as Max began to tell the chimps what they would do next.
    5. It was the best plan yet.
    6. A big chimp thumped his black chest.

2. What do you think happens next? Write sentences to continue the story.

Handwriting Practice
Trace and copy.

ch   chess   chips

che   Children like chess.

sh   she

shops   Ships still sink.

ck   trick

ick   brick

Mick has a black jacket.

The hen clucks to her chicks.

How much have you learned?

Name the picture ⟶ Write the word.

How much have you learned?

1. Write the alphabet in your exercise book in capital letters and then in lowercase letters.

2. Read the sentences. The teacher will use these sentences for dictation in your exercise book.

   Remember to start each sentence with a capital letter and finish with a period.

   1. The dog yapped at the man in the van.
   2. Bring a drink from the pack on the shelf.
   3. The quick fox ran off up the hill.
   4. Jack kicked the ball to the twins.
   5. Liz is swimming to the flagship.
   6. Bill had a chop with chips for lunch.

3. Word Search.

   Find the 30 Essential Spellings you have learned in this book.

l	o	o	k	b	a	n	y	c	m	a	d	e
a	t	h	a	t	b	c	o	u	l	d	c	d
c	o	m	e	e	f	o	r	e	g	y	o	u
w	e	h	t	h	e	i	r	i	l	i	k	e
g	i	v	e	k	l	m	n	t	h	e	s	e
c	a	m	e	o	a	b	o	u	t	p	b	y
h	a	v	e	q	t	h	e	n	r	s	h	e
s	t	t	h	i	s	u	v	w	e	r	e	w
x	t	h	e	r	e	y	z	a	b	s	e	e
m	o	r	e	c	m	a	n	y	t	h	e	y
w	h	a	t	d	b	e	c	a	u	s	e	g
m	a	k	e	b	l	i	v	e	b	h	e	r

Word race. Beat the clock.
How many words can you read in one minute?

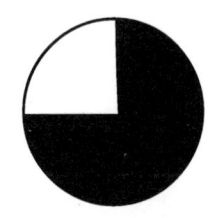

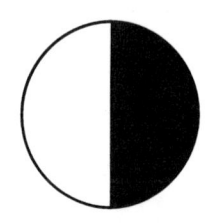

1. do	2. she	3. was	4. that	5. are
6. they	7. come	8. by	9. been	10. about
11. before	12. her	13. them	14. now	15. down
16. could	17. see	18. were	19. spring	20. thank
21. thick	22. flung	23. jacket	24. subject	25. victim
26. wigwam	27. swimming	28. twig	29. trinket	30. when
31. bacon	32. shelf	33. wanted	34. yelled	35. quick
36. why	37. dining	38. who	39. music	40. which
41. quoting	42. taxed	43. washed	44. zipping	45. cliff
46. rubbish	47. chess	48. branch	49. chicken	50. what

60 seconds	45 seconds	30 seconds
50	50	50

Certificate of Merit

presented to

_____

for the successful completion of *Reading Success Book 3*

Date _____ Signed _____ Teacher

Appendix A

Reading and Sound Cards

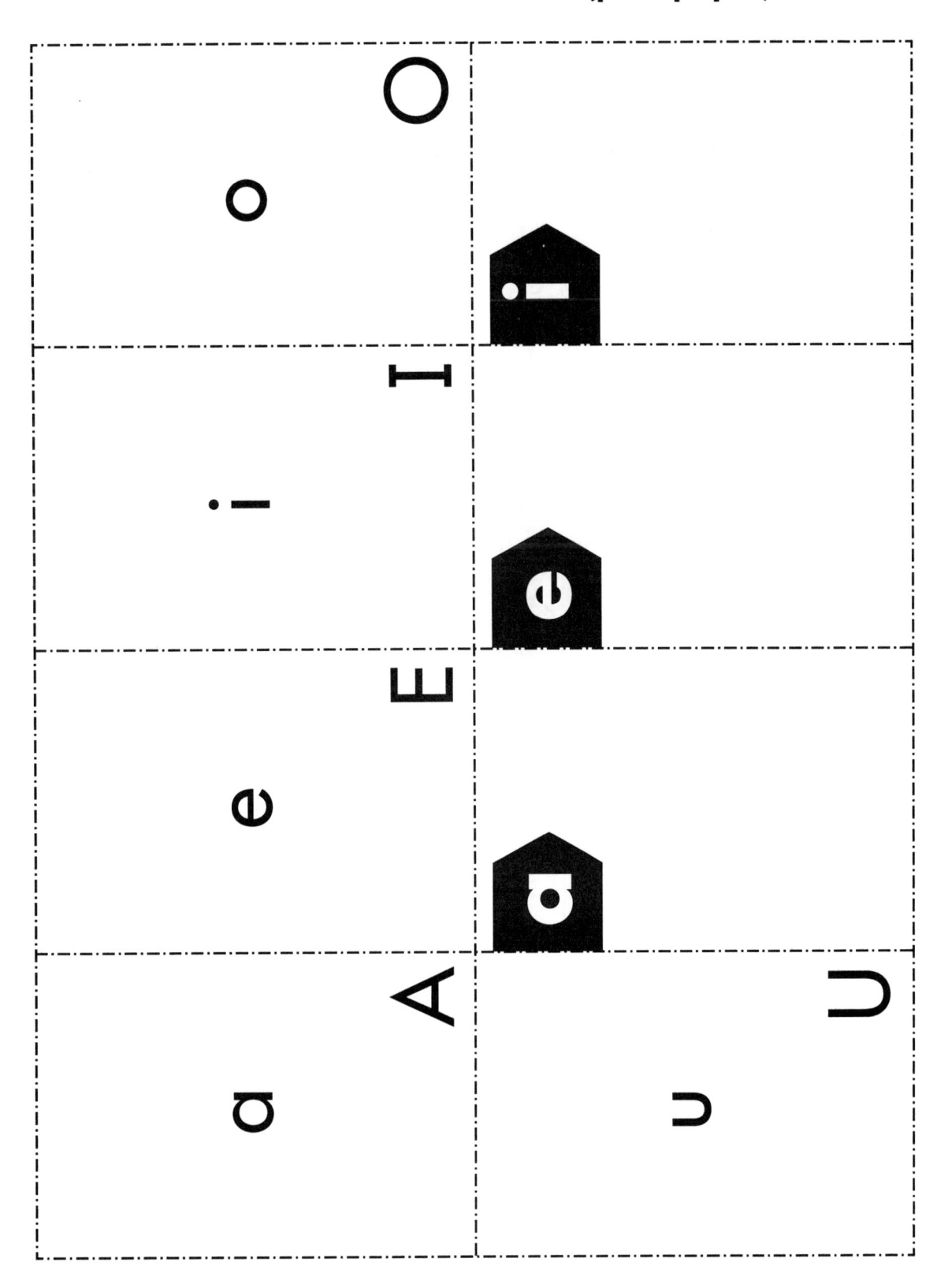

Appendix A
Reading & Sound Pictures/Spelling Pack
Vowels—Book 3—Sheet 1—Front **(pink paper)**

© LDA LL80103 *Reading Success Book 3*

Appendix A
Reading & Sound Pictures/Spelling Pack
Vowels—Book 3—Sheet 1—Back **(pink paper)**

i	open	orange
	O	**o**
e	iron	igloo
	I	**i**
a	equals	egg
	E	**a**
	acorn	apple
uniform	**A**	**a**
umbrella		
U		
u		

© LDA   138   LL80103 *Reading Success Book 3*

Appendix A
Reading & Sound Pictures/Spelling Pack
Vowels—Book 3—Sheet 2—Front **(pink paper)**

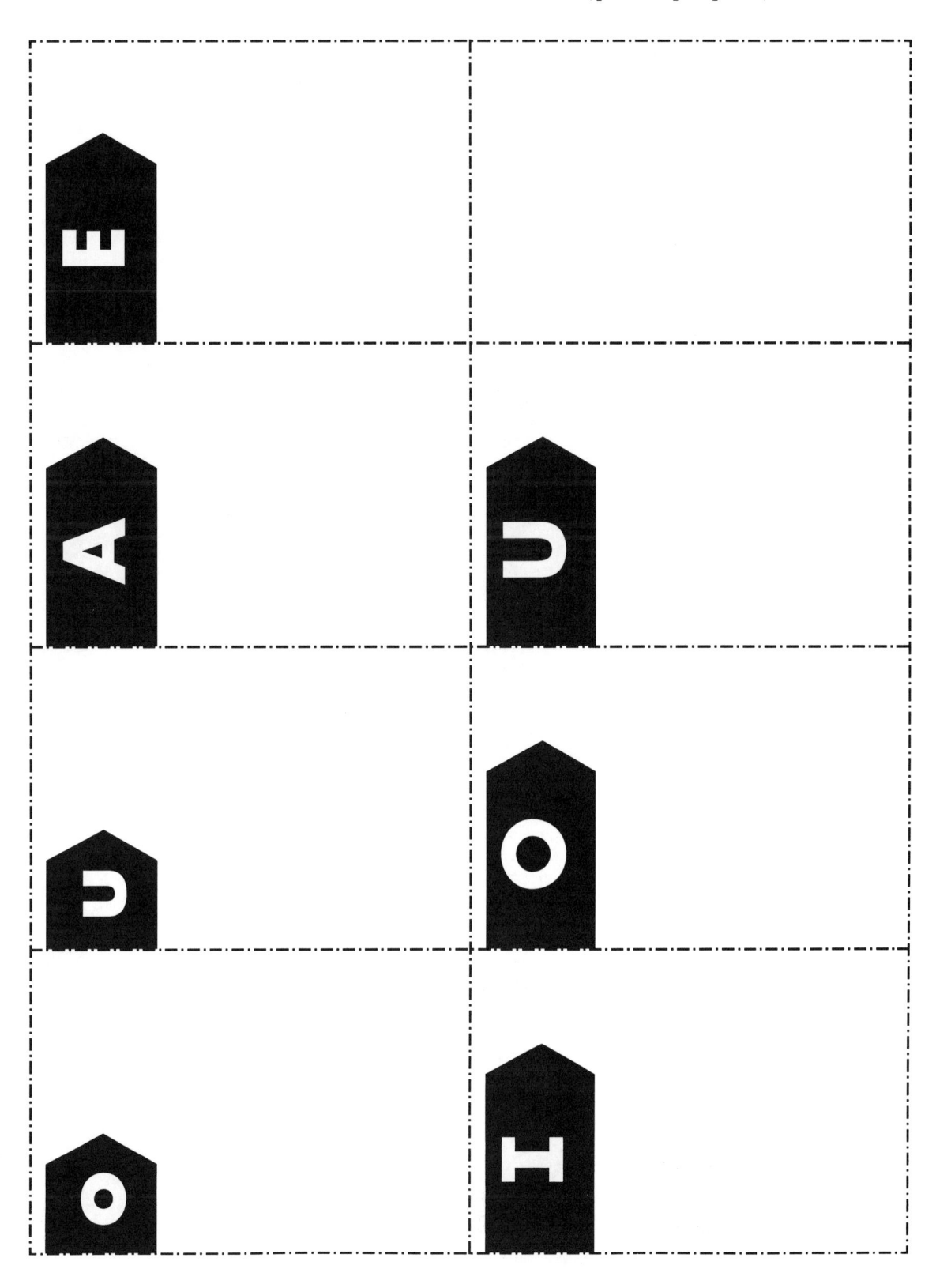

© LDA   LL80103 *Reading Success Book 3*

Appendix A
Reading & Sound Pictures/Spelling Pack
Vowels—Books 3—Sheet 2—Back **(pink paper)**

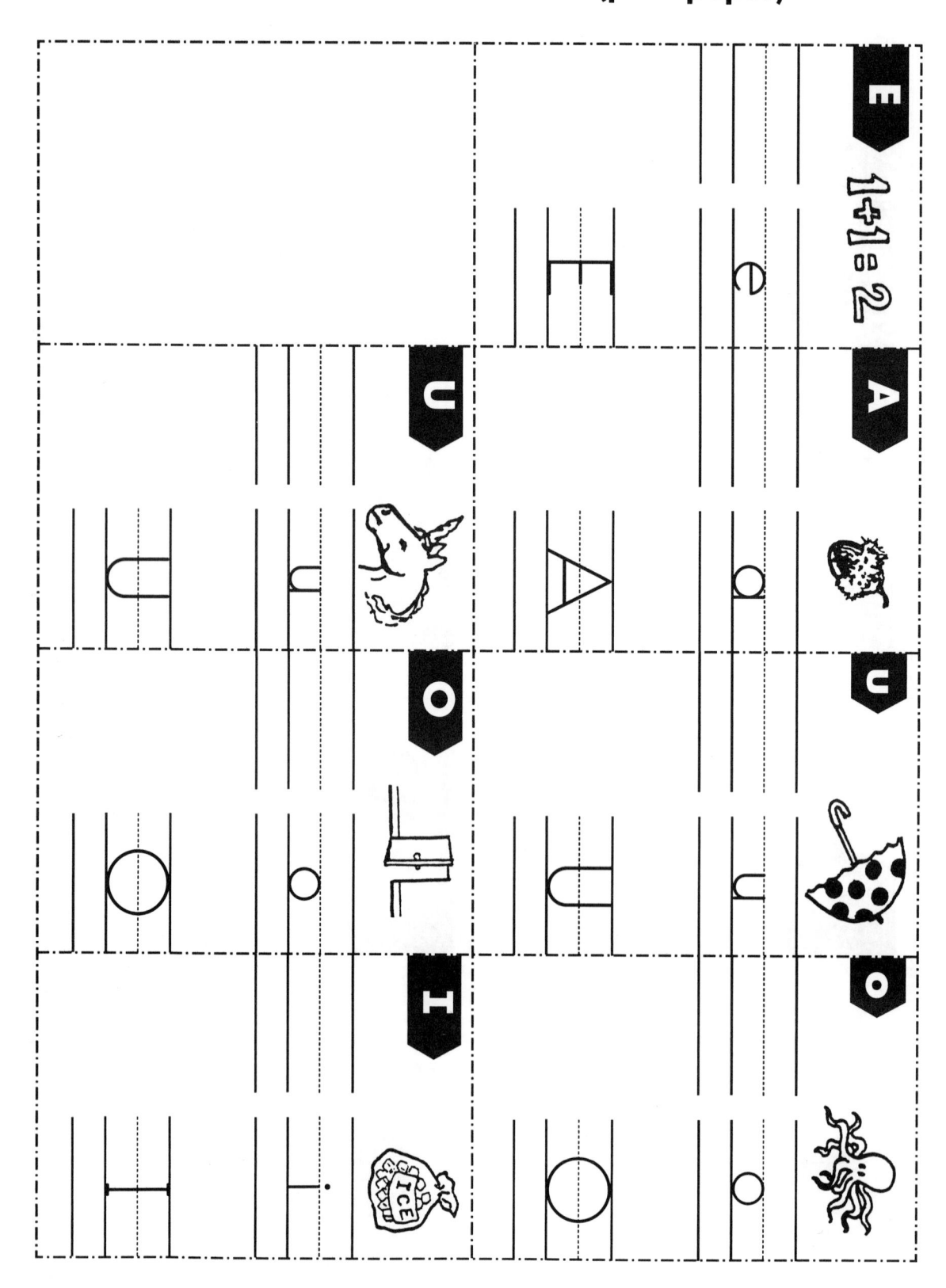

Appendix A
Reading Pack—Consonants—Book 3—Sheet 3—Front **(green paper)**

-ck / -CK	sh / SH
th / TH	j / J
-nk / -NK	w / W
-ng / -NG	v / V

Appendix A
Reading Pack—Consonants—Book 3—Sheet 3—Back **(green paper)**

duck **k**	sheep **sh**
thumb **th**	jug **j**
tank **nk**	windmill **w**
ring **ng**	van **v**

Appendix A

Reading Pack—Consonants—Book 3—Sheet 4—Front **(green paper)**

wa / WA	y / Y	qu / QU	x / X
-ed / -ED	z / Z	-ff / -FF	ch / CH

143 LL80103 *Reading Success Book 3*

Appendix A
Reading Pack—Consonants—Book 3—Sheet 4—Back **(green paper)**

cherries **ch**	box **k s**
cuff **f**	question **kw**
zebra **z**	yacht **y**
mended **ed** / yelled **d** / kicked **t**	wasp **w o**

144 LL80103 *Reading Success Book 3*

Appendix A
Reading & Sound Pictures/Spelling Pack
Consonants—Book 3—Sheet 5—Front **(green paper)**

© LDA · 145 · LL80103 *Reading Success Book 3*

Appendix A
Reading & Sound Pictures/Spelling Pack
Consonants—Book 3—Sheet 5—Back **(green paper)**

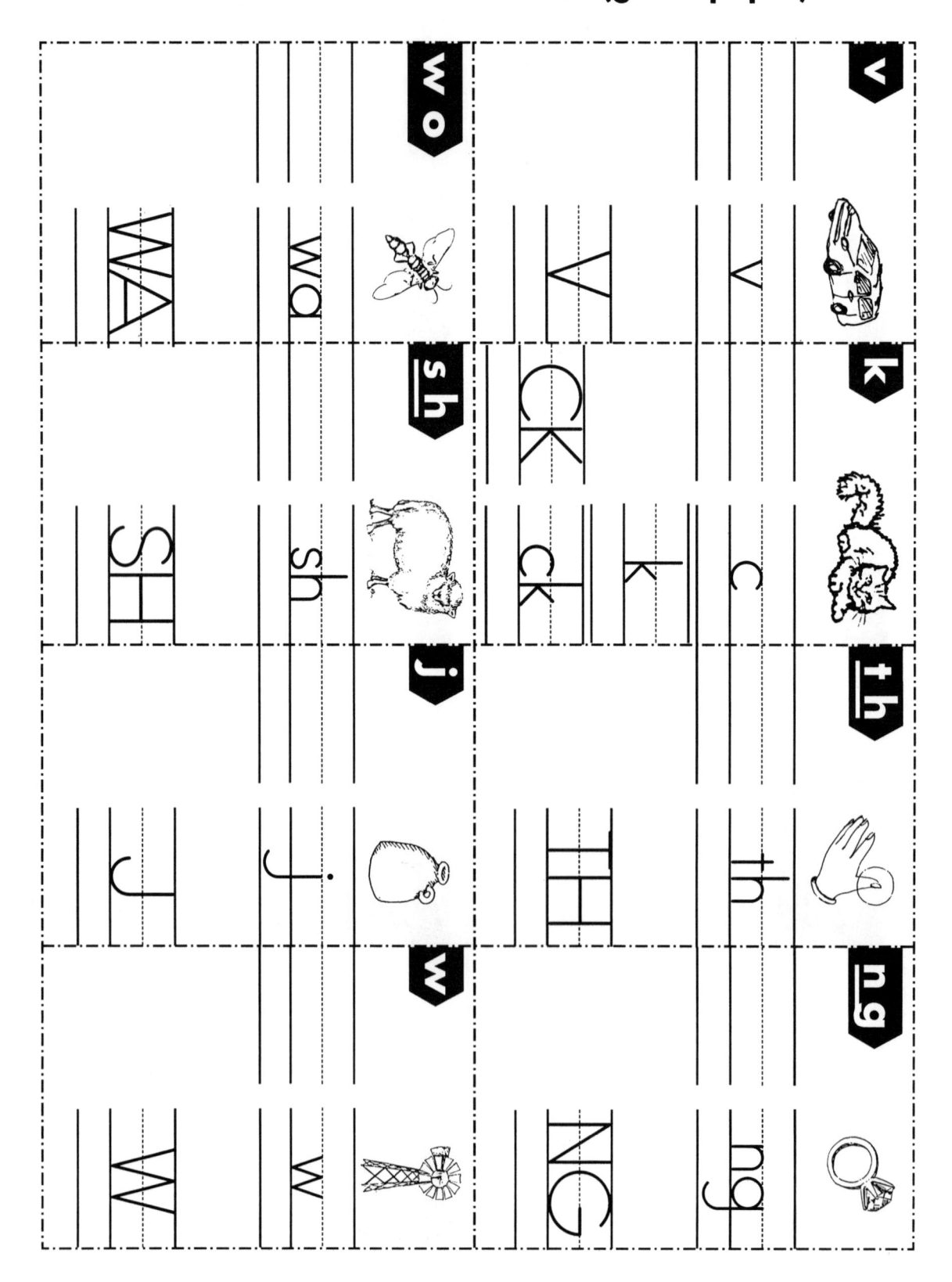

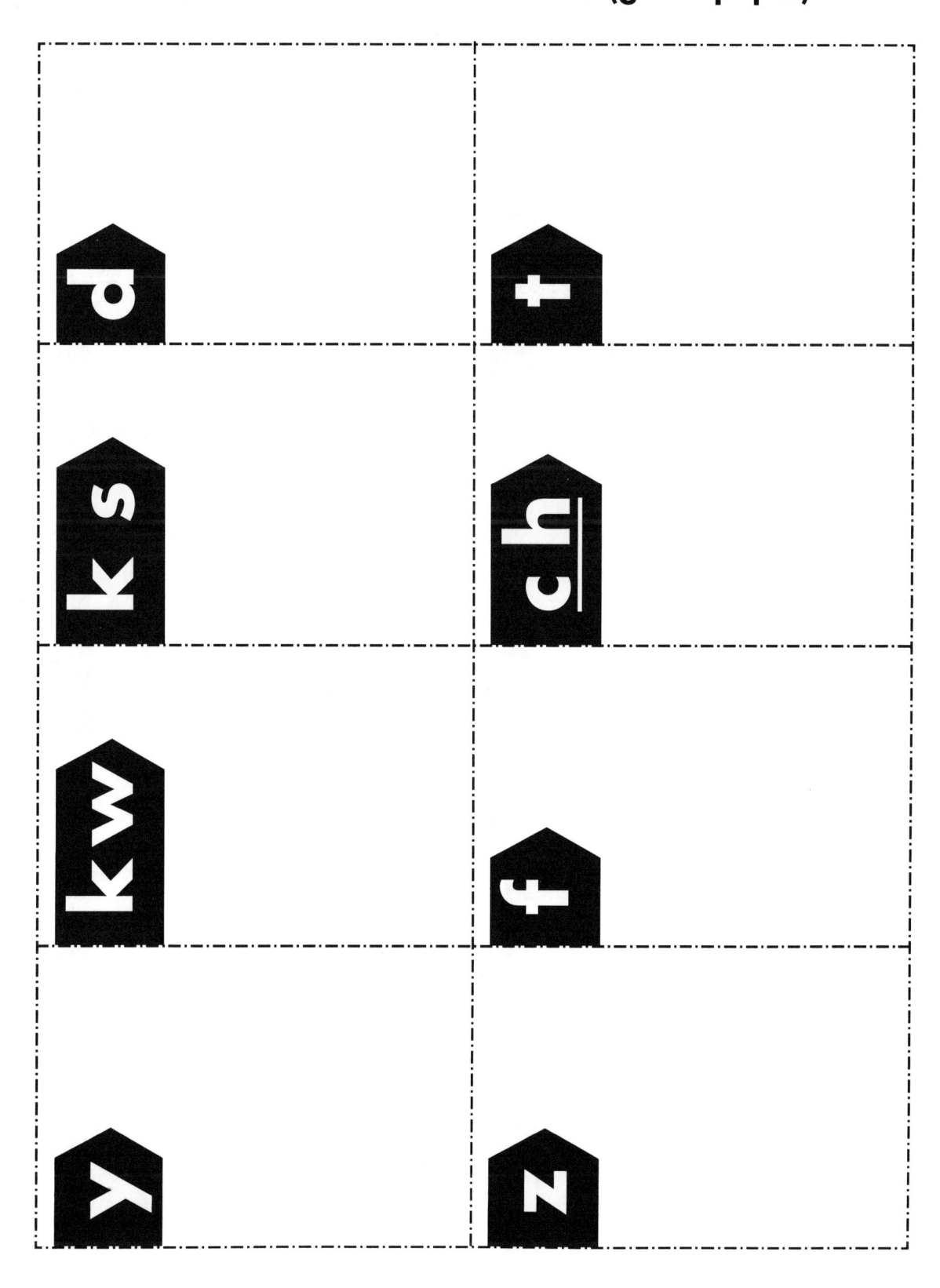

Appendix A
Reading & Sound Pictures/Spelling Pack
Consonants—Book 3—Sheet 6—Front **(green paper)**

d	t
k s	ch
kw	f
y	z

© LDA   147   LL80103 *Reading Success Book 3*

Appendix A
Reading & Sound Pictures/Spelling Pack
Consonants—Book 3—Sheet 6—Back **(green paper)**

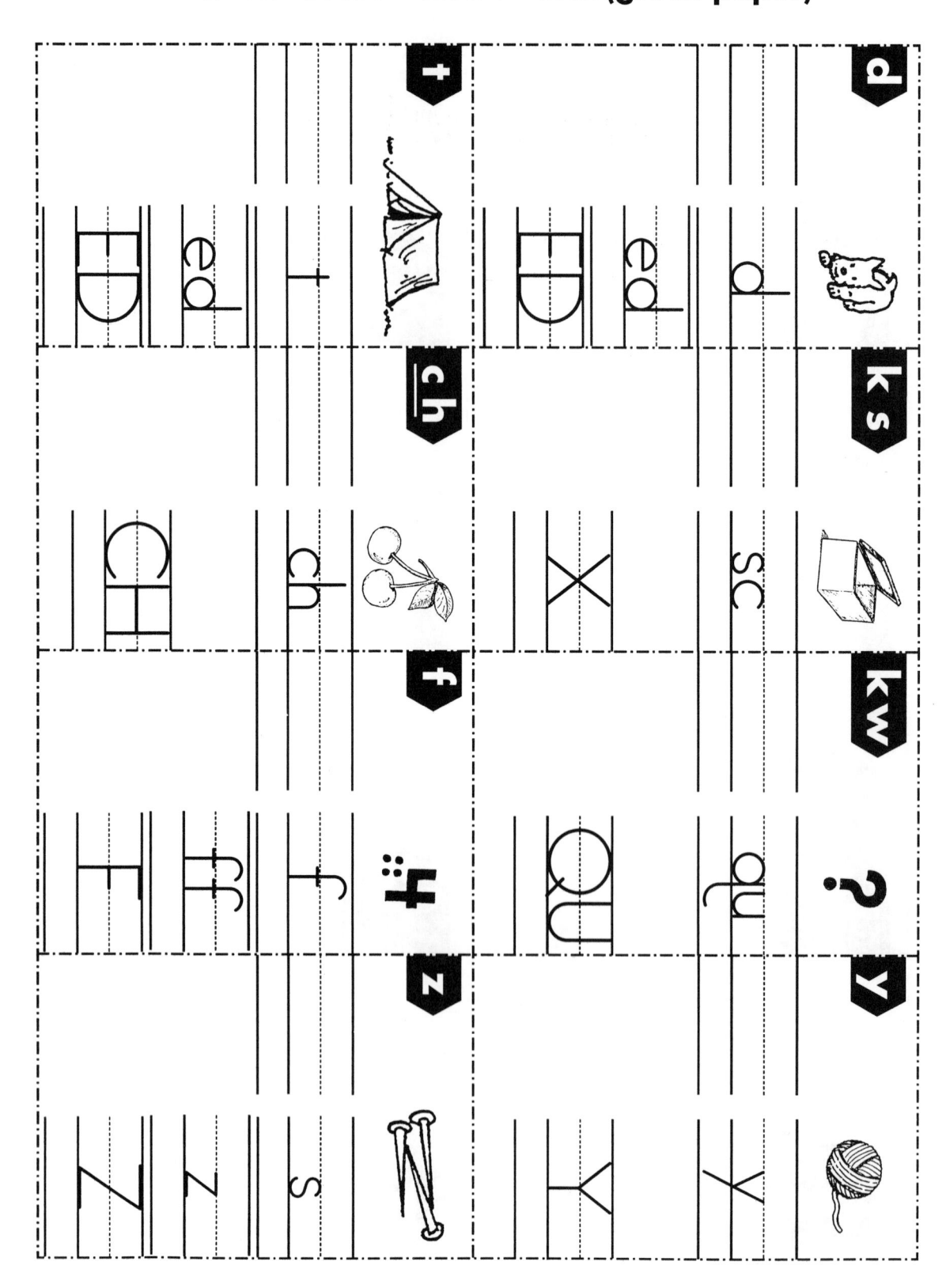

Appendix B

The following pages are reproducible flash cards to be used for drill and practice, as well as sentence building.

Make a set for each child.

After each lesson, provide the child with the appropriate word cards.

Phonetic Words

stink	sting	sink
ring	spring	sing

Phonetic Words

sang	gang	rang
long	strong	plank

Phonetic Words

helmet	bandit	admit
contest	distant	trumpet

Phonetic Words

| insect | dentist | cactus |
| magnet | fragment | suspend |

Phonetic Words

them	then	depth
think	thank	path

Phonetic Words

filming	grilling	melting
thing	cloth	resting

Phonetic Words

sank	brick	stack
lifting	sending	pick

Phonetic Words

pilot	tulip	begin
duck	black	luck

Phonetic Words

basin	van	victim
broken	open	silent

Phonetic Words

velvet	vibrant	vast
viking	vocal	invest

Phonetic Words

wax	witness	went
with	will	win

Phonetic Words

swing	swam	twigs
wing	wedding	twins

Phonetic Words

job	jet	jam
swept	twist	just

Phonetic Words

jump	yet	yell
subject	reject	unjust

Phonetic Words

yank	yak	yam
yes	canyon	beyond

Phonetic Words

clash

dash

fresh

sheep

shrub

shrimp

Phonetic Words

swamp	swan	quilt
establish	wallet	wash

Phonetic Words

request	quilt
quack	squid	grill

Phonetic Words

text	sixth	extra
box	fox	expand

Phonetic Words

frozen	cliff	gruff
zip	jazz	lazy

Phonetic Words

bunch	chomp	chop
chicken	chick	ranch

Question Words

where	why	how
who	when	what

Instant Words

come	there	could
these	this	then

Instant Words

her	for	see
come	have	that

Instant Words

like	there	after
were	about	little

Instant Words

| more | much | my |
| took | made | make |

Instant Words

because	any	many
they	she	you

CANCELED